UNLOCKING YOUR OMNIPOTENT MIND

The Essential Guide to Engineering Your Desired Reality

LUIS MANTORIS

BALBOA.PRESS

A DIVISION OF HAY HOUSE

Balboa Press books may be ordered through booksellers or by contacting:

Balboa Press
A Division of Hay House
1663 Liberty Drive
Bloomington, IN 47403
www.balboapress.com
844-682-1282

Print information available on the last page.

ISBN: 979-8-7652-4824-9 (sc)
ISBN: 979-8-7652-4826-3 (hc)
ISBN: 979-8-7652-4825-6 (e)

Library of Congress Control Number: 2023923851

Balboa Press rev. date: 01/15/2024

Legal Disclaimer

Contents

Part 2 Reality Engineering

Preface

From my personal journal:

[February 1, 2006]

"This morning marks one of the most meaningful breakthroughs I've had since I began my research. Today I woke up to new surroundings. Visually, my bedroom had the same basic appearance as when I normally wake up in it. But, not only did it have a rather unusually pleasant visual appeal to it despite the lack of change to the contents of the room, I was also experiencing a strong sense that everything had changed, or that I was finally seeing things as they had always been, but had not seen it until I woke up this morning. All of the ordinary was not so ordinary anymore. I saw how beautiful it all really was, that all of the random sounds in the atmosphere were exhilarating, and that everything I physically felt was truly remarkable. I also had the intense realization that it was all extending from me, a tangible creation of my thoughts, and that everything was as it should be, that no matter what happens, every experience was all for the best as each passing moment was leading me towards an even better and better moment. In hindsight, I know that I was looking through the eyes of my higher self, and thinking with what felt like mind that Knew its power. It was as if I had crossed a threshold and was being given (or giving myself) a glimpse of what it's like to be conscious of the ability to bring structure to the reality that surrounds me, directly from my very thoughts.

"This continued for some time until, before I knew it, I found myself back to my "usual" self. I somehow "brought myself back," so to speak, and it is obvious to me that my own subsequent thoughts of daily life and activities sneaked in to accomplish that. The experience seems to have left what feels like a permanent impression upon me. It is my strongest confirmation so far of an inner suspicion (or an inner urging) that I've had for as long as I can remember, and I intend on pursuing my research until I can master such a state of mind."

This book is the result of such research and the practices that I have undertaken for many years until the present – a book that I had originally intended to be for my own eyes only.

Introduction

This book is an essential guide to *real manifestation*. Within the context of this book, the power to manifest simply means *the ability to make something appear*, whether it be a circumstance, situation, or anything tangible, and to do so with the power of our own minds. One's omnipotent mind is supreme master of the laws governing such manifestation.

I'm not going to convince you that you have an *omnipotent mind* that has the ability to transform your reality to whatever you desire—you're going to convince yourself of that fact. The information within these pages will inspire a greater desire in you—than you already have—to find the limitless power of your mind within yourself, and you *will* find and be able to *consciously utilize* it if your desire is genuine. There are relatively few who have found it, and even fewer who, more importantly, have attained its stable realization. The information that you will find here is highly condensed and richly concentrated with regard to this subject. It does not leave you guessing as to meaning or application, but zeroes in on the essence of the subject matter, and does so in readable form.

The *omnipotent mind* is the *singular*-natured state of consciousness that emanates from the core of one's true self—the *higher self*. Singular in the sense of being unadulterated, stable, not fluctuating from pole to pole. The vibrations of *emotional energy* that are stimulated by the thoughts of the omnipotent mind, are also singular in nature. The co-creative effects of both the omnipotent mind and its accompanying emotional vibrations are of *optimal* quality and power.

On the other hand, the limited mind is the *dual*-natured state of consciousness of one's false self, the apparent lower self. The vibrations of *emotional energy* that are stimulated by the thoughts of the limited mind are also dual in nature. The co-creative effects of both the limited mind and its accompanying emotional vibrations are of *suboptimal* quality and power.

As you tried making the best out of life, trying to do everything right and following all the rules, you may feel that the results have been suboptimal, having little to show for all of your earnest efforts after so many years, leaving you unsatisfied and wanting for more. But the problem is not in what you were *(or are)* doing, but in the *type* of mind that you have been thinking *with*, along with its accompanying emotions that you maintained throughout the living of your life. The type of mind that you think with is determined by *how* you think, the meaning that you attach to everything you experience. Regardless of what you may have been taught—or by whom—you already intrinsically know that you are sovereign of your *choice* of thoughts. This is your inherent *free will*. And because you have the inescapable ability to choose where to *focus* your attention, you have the ability to think either with your omnipotent mind or with your limited mind, and thereby reap the corresponding results.

Chances are that, throughout your life, you have not made it a regular practice of continually focusing your attention with *core* thoughts and emotions that flow forth from your higher self. Neglecting to tap into your *core source* though, does not diminish the great power hidden within you, a power that you can access at any time.

It is counter-productive to resent yourself for the results in your life because resentment is just another aspect of the same lower self. Besides, it is from the platform of your lower self that you will be moving forward to greater heights. But at least you would now be aware of the work that is ahead of you, and the lower self can present many challenges for you along the way. Your power of choice can systematically overcome each one. I experienced such challenges myself. For example, at the cusp of seeing beyond the veil, I hesitated, not out of fear, but out of the realization that an enormity of difference existed between the *apparent* beingness that I was accustomed to and the *actual* beingness that lay beyond. I knew that full immersion would result in a drastic modification of the beliefs and expectations that I had adopted over so many years—beliefs that have long been so familiar to me. The mind of the lower self has a hard time admitting that it was so wrong for so long. Therefore, letting go didn't appear easy, in fact many times it felt downright brutal. Yet, having glimpsed the truth of the *Absolute*, and reaping significant benefits from such glimpses, I also knew that making the transition would be the awakening I've always sought—and one which I'm sure you seek as well. Having made the transition, you will see that what you held on to with such ferocity was actually so frail and illusory that you'll wonder why it was so hard to let go of in the first place.

* * *

The title of this book may lead some people to believe that it is about self-aggrandizement. It is not. It is about making available an active understanding of the law of mind to each unique individual user of that law, in order to guide them to a true realization of who they really are. It is also the result of over twenty-five years of my personal research, practice, and discovery of the mind's true potential.

There was a time when I resisted the thought of ever publishing the book you are now holding in your hands because it was for my own reasons that I had begun my search for the answers to questions regarding mental ability. Eventually the axiom which states *we draw to ourselves that which we resist* began to manifest, and I realized that writing this book was the right thing for me to do.

I've found that since the universe is inseparable from the mind, reality is therefore *a perpetual mental work in progress*. Not only have my prior discoveries proven to me that the mind is omnipotent, but also that all people are potential masters of reality and molders of their own destinies. To keep what I had learned to myself at a time when our spiritual evolution is rising to significant heights, would be quite an irresponsible act on my part.

The process described herein produces life-changing results. This change is dependent on your personal understanding of universal laws and the application of a connective energy which surrounds us, and which continues to amplify at a time that many are calling the *Awakening*, a passage into the fifth dimension. Such application involves the aligning of your bio-spiritual energy frequency with this higher cosmic energy frequency. That is the main impetus for my writing this book. Many people have been finding this energy to be already present in their lives to one degree or another, under varying circumstances, and due to reasons as individual as the person themself. Also, it is a foregone conclusion to me, and many others, that this energy is not only real, but is also limitless and unbounded in its capabilities.

The measurements taken of the brain-wave states of meditators and energy healers have shown an increase of gamma wave frequencies which is the highest state the brain can be in. When these frequencies are present, the mind is at its most attentive state of awareness. Whether or not an individual is able to readily attain to such higher frequencies, will be a significant determining factor of the person's ability to spiritually evolve into a conscious creator of their reality.

Relevant to the subject of brain-wave states are *belief, emotion, imagination,* and *intention.* These are covered extensively throughout this book. There is nothing wrong with the word *faith* but I don't use it in this book simply because it is a word that is so attached to religious dogma, and that fact tends to keep many people from embracing the concepts that a book like this presents. I use the words *belief* and *intention* instead. It needs to be mentioned that, just as in the use of the word *faith,* what I mean to convey is the following:

> *A sincere* choosing *of what to believe in* before *physical evidence of the chosen belief appears in consensus reality.*

This may seem quite radical or even strange to some people at first, but I assure you that very tangible results are inevitable by putting this time-honored technique into practice.

I also spare you the exhausting semantic controversy regarding terms that restrict a person's access to what they choose to believe in. This is why I emphasize *choice* as the determining factor in getting the results we seek. For instance, in Buddhism, *seeing* is superior to *believing* because, as is taught, unless you see something for yourself, what you hear or read may be false. The Christian scriptures, on the other hand, says that *faith comes through hearing,* that the Word must be heard. Embracing the former doctrine precludes the physically blind person, while the latter precludes the physically deaf person. Though I understand what they mean in the context of vibrational frequencies, most people do not make that connection. I also use the term *observer* in the context of *taking a measurement* when we are experiencing something, but the measuring and experiencing does not necessarily require physical sight or hearing. The omnipotent mind can make *true* anything whatsoever, simply by *choosing* to do so, and regardless of where the seed of the idea originated from, whether it be sight, sound, touch, etc.

It doesn't matter if you are religiously or spiritually inclined or not, your sincere practice of the methods indicated in this book will put you in a position to accomplish the seemingly impossible!

March 2016
The Author

A History of the Law – The Tablet

Hermes Mercurius Trismegistus, or *Idris*, who lived before the "great flood," was the famed author of the *Smaragdine Table*, better known as *The Emerald Tablet*. Having concealed it in a cave near Hebron, it was eventually found by Abraham's wife, Sarah. It remained in the possession of the Israelites until the days of Babylon (c. 6th century BC) where it became the possession of a Babylonian scientist-philosopher who, at his death was placed in a cave holding the tablet. In his lifetime, though, this scientist had taught Pythagoras (c. 580–c. 500 BC) who received a copy of what was inscribed on the tablet. Apollonius of Tyana (died 93 AD), who had studied the teachings of Pythagoras, obtained possession of the text. Apollonius, includes the text of the tablet in his *Book of Causes*, which has been recently translated directly from an Arabic translation into English, bypassing the Latin.

As Above So Below – These are the first words that were embossed on the original tablet, informing us of the existence of *the law of mind*. In mathematical terminology this would be called an *equation* which can be written as Above = Below. *(Notice how the equal sign (=) can easily symbolize an open-ended conduit.)* Of course, this seems to defy the "normal" laws of physics, which is why I include throughout this book an accessible explanation as to how quantum mechanics allows for this apparent contradiction. Simply put, the lofty *above* or the *superior* is another way of saying *heaven* (if you are inclined to use that term), or *where the Creator resides*. This refers to none other than the ultra-vibrational realm of the *Universal Mind*. The *below* or *inferior* would be our Earth or the tangible world where mortals reside, the world of manifestation and consensus reality. A parallel to the words of Hermes can be found in the well-known prayer that says *thy will be done, as in heaven, so on earth*, in other words *as above, so below*.

This is an indication that even Hermes long ago knew that the mind brings about our reality, and the writing of the tablet was intended to leave for posterity what he considered to be of utmost importance to him. Therefore, the teaching of our ability to access an omnipotent mind is hardly new. This book places in your hands a clear picture of this law, allowing you to understand and use it properly. There have been many interpretations of what is written on the Emerald Tablet, yet few are those that have both understood and applied them properly. The same law is also further revealed in a subsequent passage:

*The formation of the microcosm is in accordance
with the formation of the macrocosm.*

In other words, what is formed in the *subjective mind* coincides with what is formed in the *objective universe*. We can scrutinize all of the passages in detail, but the very essence of the law of mind is crystallized in those two passages. The rest of the passages symbolically represent the method of its application. This method of application is what I present to you in this book.

Thrice Hermes, a grandson of *Adam* (according to legend), in addition to being the builder of the Great Pyramid of Giza, was also considered a *representative of God*, being able to *mediate between the divine and human worlds*. He had invented a magic seal that made vessels completely airtight, hence the modern usage of the term "*hermetically sealed.*" This seal is symbolic of how it *appears* that we cannot transcend beyond the limited boundaries of reality as defined by the laws of relative physics, and that the power to do so is hidden or concealed from view, which is synonymous with the much-maligned word *occult*.

What's important to consider is the timelessness of this mental law which I refer to as a *Reciprocal Circuit*, the activity of which is hidden and concealed from view. This is the very knowledge that was maintained among the elite and within the inner circles of the most powerful and influential people in ancient civilizations. Those who were inculcated with it took vows of secrecy that carried the penalty of death if such vow were to be broken. Knowledge of this law was considered to be of utmost value, giving its possessor access to a highly coveted source of power. Such guardedness came with the intention to maintain its unadulterated purity and continuity of its teaching throughout the ages. In the hands of the greedy and the unscrupulous, countless incomplete and ineffective methods have surfaced throughout millennia. For this very reason I've placed the *examination of one's intentions* at the forefront of this book.

The law of mind is a universal law, a law that applies to all things, everywhere, at all times. Being a universal law, it is not subject to change—but change is subject to it. Everything around you exists because of this law, so it is to your utmost advantage to use it wisely. It's always been available for you to use. If you feel that your life is just the way you like it, and you wouldn't really want to change it, then you've probably been doing the right things with the law of mind all along, and I encourage you to continue doing so. For some people it is natural for them. They've learned very early on in life that the combination of certain thoughts and feelings bring about certain results. But, there's always room for improvement, room for conditions in your life to be much better than they are today. By dissolving the illusion of limitation once and for all, you can expand your creativity in so many directions. As the tablet makes clear, use of this law allows one to overcome anything whatsoever.

A Brief Overview

The Number One Obstacle to Manifestation

The most powerful reason that prevents people from manifesting their desired reality is *their fixed attention on the current undesired reality*. People that are continually unable to manifest what they desire are people that believe and feel that they are *stuck* in the reality that they are currently in. Their belief that it will continue to exist as they see it, outweighs any belief they might have about their ability to change it by using subjective processes.

The information and exercises in this book have the extraordinary effect of getting you *unstuck* and *unhypnotized* by what you can't seem to take your attention off of. However, let's cover some important basics.

There are some very key points that must be understood in order to *remove blockages of attention*, and become effective in the process of manifestation. For people that have severe blocks to their conscious ability to manifest, this understanding is crucial for them to have a manifestation breakthrough. And for people that have already tapped into that ability, this understanding will even have them producing their desired manifestations a lot faster.

Key One: The Proper View of Time

One unit of *Planck time* is the smallest unit of time that can be conceived. Named after German physicist Max Planck, the founder of quantum theory, each moment or unit of Planck time is a distinct event that exists separately from all other moments, similar to the individual frames of a film reel. Each particular moment itself does not have a direct influence in what happens in the next consecutive moment. The separate events are so close together that they appear connected, when they really are not, making it look as if it were one continuous stream. This is the illusion of the continuity of time that we experience in our physical reality.

Your ability to manifest will magnify once you truly understand the following:

It is our own thoughts that give continuity and connection to each distinct unit of Planck time, or each moment.

Key Two: The Source of Meaning

There is no actual inherent *meaning* to anything in the reality that we experience in each consecutive moment other than the meaning that *we* assign to those moments and their contents.

Key Three: The Source of Reality

The meaning that you *assign* to the contents of these distinct moments is what gives them *shape and form*. They thereby are all creations that issue forth from the observer of the particular experiences in each moment. Believing that something exists *apart* from your creation of it, tends to give it the appearance that you have no subjective control over any of the objective experiences you have.

The key to mastering your reality occurs when you break through this illusion.

Key Four: Subjective Momentum Must Be Built

Desired physical manifestations need momentum before they make their appearance. Any experience that exists in our reality only exists because it contains a *momentum of meaning* that has been built up. It is a result of having been given a consistent meaning *in a certain amount of consecutive moments*, until the reality of that experience manifested in line with the meaning that was given to it. Once it has manifested, its *continued* existence is the result of the same process.

So, each particular moment of time has its own *separate* existence from all other moments of time, and each and every moment of time can only contain the meaning that originates from the observer of those moments. This allows us to treat each moment differently by assigning whatever meaning we *choose* to assign to them. And since *giving* something meaning is what will give shape to what we are observing, we can therefore affect what happens in subsequent moments, but only after building up the required momentum.

Engineering your desired reality involves assigning *a consistent meaning to a string of consecutive moments* until a momentum builds up to the point that it takes on a life of its own. At that point, your belief and feeling about it has started to shift in your desired direction.

As the momentum continues to increase beyond the level of just belief and feeling, it also will soon bring about the tangible manifestation in accordance with your belief and feeling. Your manufactured (yet sincere) belief and feeling will then be confirmed by the existence of the manifestation itself.

To accomplish this, the meaning you choose to assign must be in line with your desired reality, regardless of what you have previously believed about the experiences you are going through in that particular string of consecutive moments.

The reason this works is because the law of attraction responds powerfully to our thoughts and feelings, and is therefore extremely instrumental in helping to build that momentum by pulling in relevant elements into the reality you are experiencing in accordance to the meaning you are assigning to it.

How many consecutive moments does it take for the momentum to build up enough for it to start to take on a life of its own? Not much. In fact, it begins with as little as twenty seconds. In twenty seconds, the attractive force of your focus builds up strong enough to begin to draw in the elements required for you to begin to believe and feel the reality of your desire. Evidence will begin to come in from a vast number of potential sources.

After about eighty seconds of being singularly focused in this manner, the pulling power of the law of attraction increases exponentially.

Building subjective momentum, though, must be done in a focused manner. Switching your attention back and forth from your desired reality to the existing reality, and so on, will not allow you to build the momentum you are aiming for.

Key Five: The Inherent Frequency of the Universe

There is a foundational, inherent frequency running through the interconnected web of the universe. This frequency consists of a continuously all-pervading state of well-being, abundance, and harmony, and it is *always* working towards an expansion of that state. This frequency is omnipresent, existing everywhere at all times, underlying the very fabric of reality. It is the fundamental essence of the creative force that permeates every aspect of existence.

This frequency influences all manifestations *to the degree that we allow it to.* As long as you are consistently aligning with that inherent frequency, and not getting in the way of it, be assured that the universe is leading you down the right road regardless of how your situation may look like. The universe is *never* fighting against you, but you must allow it to lead you out of whatever you are going through.

From the time that you begin practicing what you learn in this book, every time it appears that your experiences may not be going the way you would prefer, realizing this key will help guide you towards assigning those experiences with *optimal meanings.*

* * *

The foregoing was a basic overview of what manifestation consists of. Many specific areas will be covered in this book that also play important roles with regard to the manifestation process. Studying each area will have the serious practitioner mastering the Art of Manifestation with great precision.

PART ONE

OMNIPOTENCE FUNDAMENTALS

Chapter One

Your Desire for Power

Power tends to corrupt and absolute power corrupts absolutely.
—John Emerich Edward Dalberg-Acton (1834-1902) Historian

The desire of power in excess caused the angels to fall.
—Francis Bacon (1561-1626) Philosopher

When a mere mortal desires or claims to be omnipotent, one usually cannot help consider such a person to be quite presumptuous, to say the least. Yet, a thorough exploration of the relationship that exists between man and *the creator* will reveal that this relationship cannot be undone. It can be *forgotten*, but never dissolved. As a matter of fact, it is a permanent connection.

Often when the subject of creating your own reality comes up, the very notion of claiming to be a creator makes many people cringe. This common inclination has existed for a long time. But, our inheritance as powerful creators is undeniable, and it is at the very heart of our divine identity.

Within the mortal human frame, we exist as a primordial being that is hidden from view. Many are already discovering that this Being is who we are. When we think or become aware of something, it is this very Being that becomes aware. It is *pure awareness* or *pure consciousness. Its* ability to be aware comes from its ability to *observe.* This is the immortal, omnipotent spirit.

1

To most people, the power that exists *in potential* within us as this core spirit, seems to be inaccessible. Nothing could be further from the truth. *Omnipotence is, and always has been, readily accessible!* It is available to you at this very moment. But in order to realize omnipotence—and realize it fully—you must first allow yourself to access the *qualities* of the spirit.

It is the very root of life itself because if everything were to be stripped from It—the body, the environment, and so on—It is the irreducible existence that will continue to independently remain. It is the *essential* part of life itself.

As the spirit starts to take part in the material universe, and experiences it in a physical body, it is bombarded with *effects* from all directions—*the effects of its own creation*. It then erroneously considers these effects as having a causative nature. It *chooses* to view them as *a* cause of its experience. It is this very process which keeps obstructing our memory of our own true inherent quality as causative spiritual beings, thereby believing ourselves to be effects of these apparent "causes." The exposure to these highly convincing effects prompts the spirit to believe things that are foreign to its nature, such as "this happened *to* me," "*they* made me feel like this," "I was *destined* for this," and so on. We have handed over the scepter of our divine nature and have assigned other authorship to externalities. Thus the connection to this omnipotent mind has been forgotten. Of course, this did not happen overnight. It took many physical incarnations throughout the ages to reduce us in this way. So, it would only serve to continue to suppress our spiritual native abilities when we continue to believe that our oneness with divinity is excessively pretentious. We are capable of reversing the downward process.

In order to adopt this most important basic quality, you must first believe the following:

I Create my own Reality - Knowingly or Unknowingly

If the above is true, you may ask, then what is it that the spirit is capable of? What does or can it *cause*? In one word—*everything!* Yes, you read that correctly. It can produce or change any condition, object, or circumstance that can ever exist. This is the reason ancient wise men have called it *the All*. We have a divine inheritance that has no limitations. If it did, then it wouldn't have its root in the divine. It is *absolute cause* which *causes absolutely*.

Expressing omnipotence begins with the spirit operating through the mind. The spirit has no boundaries when it comes to what it can accomplish with the mind. And in such boundless state, the mind expresses itself with its omnipotence. But we prevent ourselves from realizing this expression whenever there is resistance in the form of suboptimal beliefs. These beliefs in turn give birth to vibrational patterns that are contradictory to the pure vibrations that emanate from the qualities of spirit. One of these beliefs that act as a barrier from accessing the mind's omnipotence is the belief that the mind is susceptible to limitations, that it has a limited scope of ability. The truth is that there are no actual limits or boundaries to mental power. As a matter of fact, the illusion of limits is itself a mental creation which can be undone. That is one of the first things this book will help you realize.

To obtain a position of power has always been one of the most sought after goals in life. Many dream of having the ability that would allow them to be in control of events and circumstances in their lives. This pursuit is complicated by the fact that there are many degrees and facets of power. Ask several people what power is and you'll get several different answers. One will say *money* is power, while another will say *knowledge* is power, yet another says *political influence, physical prowess, possession of firearms,* and so on. The power these grant reside in the realm of limitations, not in the realm of *true* power.

The desire for power stems from the basic fear of being helpless in one way or another. Power is basically the ability to act or produce an effect. The fear of not being able to produce effects

3

can range from not being able to put food on the table to not being able to conceive a child, or from not being able to ward off bullies at school to not being able to rid oneself of a horrible infirmity.

Ask yourself: *what would life be like if I had the power to bring about anything in my life?* Would you want that kind of power? If so, why? What things would you do? What would you do first? Would you have to think up a list of things to accomplish or would you naturally know what to do? I ask you the foregoing questions purposely because these are issues that surface for many people when they make the discovery of what the mind is truly capable of.

Two of the inner issues I dealt with concerned my priorities and my personal responsibility with what I referred to as "unexpected collateral results." I had gotten rid of the fear of helplessness only to be confronted with the fear of the changes that would unknowingly occur as a consequence of engineering my own reality. Then I realized that change is all around us all the time, unavoidable, and that everything changes, and that part of being a conscious creator of your own reality involved doing away with such a fear. A basic understanding and acceptance of change will make it easier for you to embrace the nature and range of your ability to direct these changes at will.

Omnipotence means *all-power,* and in using that term I mean just that. We have within our reach the power to accomplish absolutely anything at all. If you really think about it, wouldn't this change just about everything in terms of how you view your life and everything around you? Yes it would, and all for the better, if approached properly. I say this because, the closer you come to the full potential of spirit, there will be an inevitable accompanying increase of responsibility that will reach a level of meaning beyond your present concept of the word. Cause and responsibility will become synonymous terms to you. Don't ever think that you can escape responsibility for anything that you do. That is another illusion. As a matter of fact, your scope of responsibility encompasses a whole lot more than you may have ever been willing to accept.

Within the omnipotent mind there has always been contained *the solution to any problem that could ever exist.* Whatever problem you may have, the solution is right there available—*always has been.* Above all, you have every right to lay claim to this power which has always been yours. Therefore, allow nothing and no one to inhibit or deny you your rightful inheritance.

You've Been Giving Your Power Away

Omnipotence has always been available to us. If this is true, where has it been all of our lives? You may ask why you haven't seen nor experienced it in your own life. *I most certainly would have seen something confirming its existence by now* you may say. Yet you *have* seen it! The problem lies in the fact that you've been giving your power away without you even realizing it.

Due to human nature, we are not in the habit of taking significant responsibility for our lives and the world we live in. Whenever we do acknowledge responsibility, it is mostly superficial and rarely meaningful. *Blame* is what is most rampant among us. Being locked into this mindset assures our estrangement from our omnipotent mind. Under the blame mindset, everything else causes this or that, something or someone else is always the source or origin of whatever happens around us. Whenever we do say "I did it," we're usually saying that we *physically* went through the motions of doing something. We therefore don't really mean *I* did it, because the true I, or the spirit that is who you are, is the *you* from the realm of Unlimited Power—not your body nor your name, which are creations existing in the realm of limitations. The true *you* is the true source of everything you experience. We unknowingly deny this because, on a certain level of thinking, to accept responsibility for so much of what is called evil around us, and to acknowledge that we are the cause of it is to also affirm the imperfection created by a Mind that should have no flaws. I say *on a certain level of thinking* because this thinking is based on a *dual* mind, a *judgmental* mind that has no place in an omnipotent mind. This is because the moment Divinity looks at Itself and says that it is wrong, it demotes Itself and immediately begins to lose sight of its true power. It drops down even further when it claims that, not only does something *defective* exist, but *someone or something else* brought it about. That is where the state of most of humanity has been for a very long time. This is considered "normal" and even "acceptable" by most. Yet, very recently our own science has been disproving this very notion.

Examine Your Intentions

You've heard that *power in the wrong hands is dangerous*. I would go further and say that power in the wrong hands is *primarily dangerous to the very individual wielding that power*. The people I've seen try to use this power as a bow and arrow have watched their arrow in mid-air transform into a gigantic boomerang of which there seemed to be no escape. The reason this will invariably happen is because whatever you intend for the universe, you also intend for yourself. The oneness of the universe includes you as well.

So, try as you may, the attempt to use the techniques I provide in this book with a mind of duality which manifests separation, vengeance, hatred, jealousy, and so on, will end up backfiring upon you.

Accessing your omnipotent mind involves a transformation of how you look at yourself and the universe around you. This transformation will very well be the most significant change that you will ever experience because it will change everything else in your life. The type of change that occurs will depend on what your *intentions* are for acquiring and using this power. Are you willing to abandon views that have only limited the scope of your abilities, or do you find letting go of such beliefs too much for you to handle? For instance, you may presently believe that one of your neighbors is evil, that your future is bleak, or that you could never forgive yourself or others for the things in the past. All of these things, though, are *thoughts, beliefs* and *emotions* that are malleable and can be modified to your benefit, but unless you are willing to believe more in your power to create your reality, changing those situations will continue to elude you.

Therefore, as you will learn more in detail later on, everything in existence is a mental creation of the very *mind* that we have access to. In order to improve this mental creation, you must be willing to change how you think and feel. These changes must be done by your power of *choice*, not on the strength of some other "source" outside of yourself.

Whatever You Want is Obtainable

Many people have been prompted by their view of the global economic situation to seriously consider their priorities. This involves taking a very good look at the things that you consider important to have in your life. There are things "missing" in everyone's life that would make living life easier and more fulfilling. You know what they are, but what you may not know is *how* to obtain them. It's time that you started doing a refocus on what your true priorities should be!

Despite the *appearance* of lack and loss, there is an abundance of prosperity and opulence available to *each* of us at *all* times. That abundance will be there regardless of whether you try to figure out *how* to realize it in your life or not. If you unleashed your imagination and allowed yourself to indulge your thoughts in the things you never thought you could have, I'm sure that you could list about a million things. Knowing what you want is important because it helps you tap into the vibrational frequencies that become available as you focus on what you desire. But it is even more important to understand that staying away from the *how* will actually expedite the manifestation of the items on your own list.

To help spark your imagination, I've provided below a sample list of popular things many people start their lists off with. Modify it as needed. Remember, omnipotence means that there is no limit to what can be done.

° A Million Dollars °

° A Successful Business °

° Perfect Health °

° Perfect Vision °

° A Full Head of Hair °

° A Date with a Model °

° A Happy Marriage °

° Pleasant Neighbors °

° A Large (Paid Off) House °

° Peace and Security °

° Artistic Talent °

° Athletic Ability °

° An Athlete's Body °

° Superior Strength °

° The Loss of Excess Weight °

° Ability to Speak Other Languages °

° A Beautiful Voice °

° Good Looks °

° A Billion Dollars °

Take your time creating your list. You'll discover that some things are what you consider true *needs*, while others are merely *wants*. Your sense of priority will kick in, as well as your sense of responsibility. What you don't want to do is introduce the *How* of obtaining certain items on your list. Let go of any thoughts that indicate that you may be responsible for something wrong happening if you were to get what you want. In other words, if, as you intend to manifest something, there is an *accompanying belief* that the manifestation will harm someone in some way, you are actually in the process of mixing vibrations that will affect the result of your creative process. This reminds me of the often-told story of a man who wished to become rich, and did so not long after his wish. The downside was that the riches came to him as the inheritance proceeds from the passing away of a relative. The limiting belief that *"the available inheritance is the only way feasible to attain such riches"* is a likely cause of such a result. Don't underestimate the power that comes with the proper use of the law of mind. Depending on the degree of how much you let go of the *how*, and refrain from concerning yourself with possible undesirable side-consequences, so will the speed of your manifestations occur along with the least amount of what you consider to be undesirable side-consequences.

Until I realized this myself, my fear of being responsible for the collateral results I was forecasting was something I struggled with. I had reasoned with myself that I didn't want to get what I wanted regardless of what else may happen. Intention will involve not only your thoughts, but also the feeling and meaning that *accompany* those thoughts. Because of this, any fear you may have will result in its own effect as well. On the other hand, a person believing that he will cause harm, though having no fear, but proceeds in the delight of seeing such a result, will eventually have an adverse result rebound against himself. This is why it is so important to *acknowledge that you are causatively connected to all of life*. This may not be clear to you at the moment, and to some of you it may even be an annoying thing to hear. But I assure you that in the process of adopting this basic understanding, you will be safeguarded against yourself, thereby saving yourself a lot of heartache.

Being sure and clear about what you want without the need to know *how* it will enter your experience, is a necessary step in obtaining it. Be thorough with your list and go over it several times. Revise it if you need to as you go through this book. Prioritize it from *most important* to *least important*, and if it helps to *categorize* the items of your list, do so. By the time you reach the chapters dealing with technique, you won't struggle much with what to apply the technique to.

As you look at the entirety of your list, realize that it represents a fraction of what you previously considered to be an "impossible world." It'll just be a matter of time before you reach the conclusion that *nothing is impossible for you*.

Exercise One

The following exercise assists you in remembering that You are the creator of your reality. You may already know this *theoretically* from what you have read so far, or from what you have been inspired to believe. But, this exercise goes further. It helps you to actually experience and train yourself to develop the mindset that allows you to consciously use the law of attraction in a way that allows you to *deliberately create your desired reality*. It is important to master each step, so whenever you progress to a subsequent step, make sure that your focused and uninterrupted practice of that particular step lasts for at least fifteen minutes.

[*This exercise can be done at any time. It is recommended, though, that your first few sessions be conducted when you are not engaging in an activity that demands your immediate attention. As you progress, you can expand the practice of the exercise during other activities, as long as you can do so while successfully accomplishing the exercise.*]

1. *Listen* to all of the sounds around you, *look* around your environment or outside your window and *watch* all the movement and events that occur. The key to this exercise is to *witness everything with no particular judgment on your part in any particular direction.*

2. As sounds and events unfold, continue holding the attitude of an *interested observer.* Realize that events *must* unfold, and that events *will* appear in your field of experience. It might be your next interaction with someone that either approaches you where you are, or calls you on the phone. From where you are right now, come to the strong realization that something yet unknown to you *will* happen, and you choose ahead of time to not let it affect you, and that you will form no opinion about it, but that you accept it as it comes. From this position you are giving yourself the opportunity to gently *step back and observe* what is occurring without becoming enmeshed in the event in an emotionally adverse manner.

3. As soon as something enters your field of awareness, you may notice that certain unwanted *feelings* will begin to try to emerge, and you will notice that these feelings have a very intimate connection with unwanted sensations that also surface within your physical body. *Maintain the same attitude of an interested observer even as you experience these feelings and sensations.* All of these physical bodily sensations are manifesting as the result of a momentum that your prior thoughts and beliefs have produced. Continue to realize that as *observer,* you have the choice to view whatever you observe in a negative way or in a positive way. It was the mind that *chose* to feel disturbed, and it is mind that can also choose to view the situation in a way that will by necessity be accompanied by a more acceptable emotion. This is the *Art of Transmutation.*

Maintain your position as observer and allow yourself to view these sensations in a detached and unaffected way *as if you were viewing a separate personality that was experiencing those feelings,* instead of yourself. Resolve to be undisturbed come what may. The reason the unwanted feelings surface is because the mind is making connections established by prior patterns of thought. This exercise makes you aware of the mind's ability to establish any new pattern that it *chooses* to establish. Whatever your *I* consciousness can become aware of, it has the ability to adjust ahead of time how it will view it in terms of meaning and feeling.

Just like a movie projector, what you perceive as your experiences are projections, except that the experiences that you are projecting will adjust in accordance to your *view* of them, in other words, *how you consider* those experiences. This phenomenon occurs because *your beliefs, expectations, and the feelings you feel are not only part of the projection, but have a powerful influence on the entirety of the projection!* By performing this exercise properly, you will allow yourself to notice the difference between being the *projection* as opposed to being the *projector*. By changing your position you change your power status.

Receive your every incoming experience as they come to you, all the while maintaining a sense of interest, and without being distracted by any uncomfortable emotions that may try to intrude. Harboring fear will only bring to your life more of what you fear.

Maintaining *expectant interest* will bring to you what genuinely interests you. If what you normally consider a dangerous situation begins to present itself to you, then use wisdom and common sense while maintaining your composure, but keep in mind that such an unwanted situation is also a manifestation of what you have previously entertained subjectively. Such an experience only shows up by means of a previously-built momentum that was already in place.

4. As you maintain your position as an interested observer, your next step will be to realize that nothing that you are observing is appearing by chance, but *it is all a very precise reflection of you!* Every detail that you experience is a product of the thoughts and feelings you are constantly emitting in real time. Sincerely acknowledge that you are the cause of the event, but never with a feeling of guilt for anything that may happen.

As you continue anticipating your next experience, accept the fact that whatever ends up occurring is a manifestation that you are responsible for creating. Until you do so, you will continue to remain blind about the restructuring of the experiences you have. Change is going to happen whether you want it to or not. You have the power to determine what those changes will be by the subjective qualities you *deliberately attach* to those changes, as opposed to merely having uncontrolled reactions to them. You won't be able to do this until you rise above the events that have a grip on the emotions that limit you. Your comfort-zone will expand dramatically in all directions because your fear of unexpected experiences will be seen for what it really is—your own mental creation that perpetuates the very things you fear.

Continue to persist in knowing that situations will come your way that *seem* to be out of the blue. They are not. For every effect there is a cause, and *you* are that cause. Being aware of and accepting these as *your* effects in a consciously controlled manner is the first step to recognizing your causative nature.

The *regular* practice of this exercise must be continued in order to adjust mentally to this new way of viewing life events, and in order to become effective in your use of the *law of attraction*. It soon will become apparent to you how deeply immersed you were in the fear of the unknown, and how much your understanding and tolerance of change has skyrocketed.

*Note: The above exercise may seem to implement an unusual way of thinking, but the usual way of looking at the world is a veil which leaves one quite impotent compared to what can be done when the illusions that are blindly accepted as truth are penetrated. Our true potentialities are easily hidden from us when we interpret, define, and label what our senses reveal to us in a way that gives our power away, resulting in suboptimal results in our lives. But when looked at from the perspective of our true creative nature, and from the stance that our true being embodies, the changes that occur around us become better experiences that lead to even much better experiences, continually making provisions that are in line with our most-desired intentions.

Chapter Two

The Reciprocal Circuit

True power is obtained with the proper use of the mind. The reason for this is because, just as there is a *physical sphere* that encompasses the entire universe, there exists a *mental sphere* which is inextricably linked to that same universe. The mind is ever active in this mental sphere, which in turn is having an effect upon the physical sphere at all times.

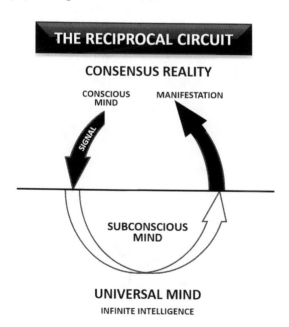

THE RECIPROCAL CIRCUIT

CONSENSUS REALITY

CONSCIOUS MIND   MANIFESTATION

SIGNAL

SUBCONSCIOUS MIND

UNIVERSAL MIND
INFINITE INTELLIGENCE

This connection is what enables the mind to be the most powerful mechanism we have at our disposal because absolutely anything that can possibly originate in the mind, can be put into effect, or manifest, in our physical universe. The ever-present *circuit* which acts as a conduit between the mind and reality is *The Reciprocal Circuit*. Let me simplify how this circuit works:

The Cosmic Mirror

The Reciprocal Circuit is similar to a mirror. The basic purpose of a mirror is to reflect back to us our own image when we look into it. This is exactly what takes place when we look all around us in our day-to day lives. *Every* experience we have is a reflection back to us of our very selves. There is no exception to this. All the sounds you hear, the things you see and feel, all the circumstances you encounter, even these words that you are reading at this very moment are *aspects of yourself reflected back at you.*

The adoption of the above concept is crucial to your safe and effective application of the power of your mind. If you eliminate the belief that you are separate from your life experience by replacing it with the view that everything around you is an *extension* of your own being, it won't be long before you start realizing how senseless it is to cause harm or attach negativity to anything. If you do, you would be harming yourself in the process. That is the mirror's warning label.

Effectively applying this power is possible because since everything is an extension of yourself, then you are the one making it all happen to begin with, knowingly or unknowingly. Though it can be applied at will, you won't be able to do so unless you come to grips with the fact that the world around you, and everything you experience as an individual, is your very own personal mirror, a conduit that reciprocates exactly what you put into it. You can either smile, cry or yell into it, but one thing is for sure—*you will get back exactly what you put into it.* This may be your very first awareness of the presence of the mirror, nevertheless it's always been there.

Take a good look around you. It is time to start realizing that all of your deepest convictions, judgments, thoughts and emotions are embodied in the world you've been experiencing, and *are* experiencing. This, thereby, makes you the *engineer* of your own reality. You just never knew how powerful you truly are, and you may still have difficulty accepting this concept, but if you truly want to unlock the power within you to consciously change your world, you must start to look at everything with a new pair of eyes. You'll need to fully embrace the connection you have with all there is before you can consciously exercise true power.

The One Omnipresent Mind

The entire universe is a vast mental creation made up of consciousness. The mind that creates it is *indivisible,* though it can be *conceived* of as being divisible. This is when someone says "you have your own mind, and I have mine." We do have our own *states* of mind at any given moment, and we also have our own *decisional* power, the power to *choose,* but these are functions of that *one mind.* Trying to divide the mind in such a way would only succeed in hiding the mind's true unity from the individual making such conception. There exists only one true Mind, and it is everywhere. It has been referred to as the Mind of the *All.* What we have come to know as individually separate minds are *aspects* of this one great Mind, just as drops of water in the ocean are parts of the entire ocean. The only thing separating "your" mind from this one omnipresent, universal mind is your *belief* in that very separation. Begin recognizing that there is only one omnipresent mind, believing in its actuality, and you immediately activate your potential mental influence.

We are at all times thinking *within* this one mind. To help you come to the realization of this concept, consider an invisible substance pervading the entire universe. This is *mental substance*. Now consider that your very thoughts and feelings also consist of this invisible substance which is an actual *extension* of yourself. Every time you think and feel, you do so within this vast sea, and it will respond to all of your intentions. No matter where you place your awareness within this sea, one point within it can instantaneously reach any and all other points within it that correlate with its intention in order to create any effect whatsoever, including the receiving of remote information. This will occur not only regardless of distance, but also regardless of time. So it goes with any other person who thinks within it. Every person exists and thinks within this same mind.

When you reduce your belief of having this one mind, you operate only within the framework that you have limited yourself to. A "separated mind" by definition has already limited itself. It believes it can only do so much, and therefore only does so much. If it believes that it can't, then it won't. If it believes that it isn't, then it won't be. This is akin to a man with perfect vision who has blindfolded himself, forgot that he did so, and believes himself to be physically blind.

Since the entire universe is a creation of this one mind that we think into, there is nothing that we cannot change within it. Disease, for instance, would be understood as a mental creation that can be made to disappear by intending health, regardless of who has the disease. If "their mind" put it there, then "another mind" intending or having the knowingness of health and vitality within the one universal mind for that "diseased" individual, can undo the existence of the disease because it is of the same mental substance that created it to begin with. The mirror will reflect back the person's health as it is put forth. The powerful divine qualities present within the omnipotent mind will not see such imperfection in its universe. The awareness of this perfect intention can only manifest a healthy reality for such a person. Though such diseases are not necessarily desirable things to have, they appear mainly when an underlying premise has somehow, directly or indirectly, been established in the mental realm that allows it to manifest. Such a premise is one that is easily "passed on" to others when it is based on our societal belief system. The mind placed it there, and it is the mind that also has the power to remove it by viewing the desired state.

This basic concept is important for you to understand and accept in your life in order to bring about the results you desire. This is the foundation of your omnipotent mind, a mind that knows no boundaries.

The Aspects of Mind

The aspects of mind found in the mental sphere, consists of the conscious, subconscious, and the super-conscious levels of awareness. We are very familiar with the conscious mind for it is our own awareness. The *subconscious* mind, on the other hand, is a term which is often misused. When access to the subconscious mind is accomplished, it is done using the qualities of the *lower self.* Super-consciousness is what we access using the qualities of the *higher self.* It is what makes possible our *desired* manifestations— it is the key to unlimited power. The super-conscious and subconscious aspects of the mind know no boundaries and accept everything the conscious mind places its attention on. The end result depends on the quality of what the mind focuses on. These aspects of the mind are of the very substance that makes up the universal mind. So, how do these aspects operate?

I refer to the basic function of these two aspects as *The Reciprocal Circuit* because it is just that: *a circuit whose main function is to reciprocate.* You "send," or better stated, *emanate* a current of information along this circuit, and the signal is given back to you in equal measure. You get exactly what you give, nothing is for free.

Now, the information emanated can be anything that the conscious mind can conceive or be aware of. This will then become accepted by either the super-conscious or the subconscious aspect of the mind, which in turn presents it to you in your life experience. We never see the inner workings of these aspects of the mind because such vibrational frequencies are beyond our physical reality field of awareness—but we do see their results.

These aspects of mind are part and parcel of the *Universal Mind*, and your particular involvement in it is your individual mentality within that universal mind. Your *involvement*, or never-ending access to it allows you to reach any part of it faster than the speed of light, instantaneously. Anything that was, is, will be, and *can* be, at any point in time and at any place, exists and is available to you within the universal mind!

Super-consciousness is *omnipresent*, though by its very nature it is also *invisible*. It actually permeates all of existence beyond the ability of our physical senses to perceive it. The powerful results we obtain are incontrovertible proof of its existence. We know and recognize it by the effects it produces. The only way we can see what's inside of it is by pulling something out of it into manifestation.

The above is a very basic explanation of how this mental circuit works. To illustrate, I'll share with you my very first experiment with regard to the power of the super-conscious mind. It involved something simple, but yet not so simple that I could brush it off as a coincidence. It involved an orange. I decided to have the super-conscious mind produce an orange for me in a very specific way. I chose an orange because at that moment, I couldn't remember the last time I had seen one. I knew I had none in the house, so I performed a specific visualization technique which involved a hand bringing an orange into my house. I decided not to put a face on whoever that person may turn out to be. Afterwards I just went about my business, forgot about the whole thing and went to bed.

Being a night-owl in those days, I always woke up after 10:00 a.m., but that morning I unexpectedly woke up much earlier, 5:30 a.m. to be exact. What I couldn't understand was that I felt as if I had gotten a full night's sleep when I had only slept for barely three hours, and there was nothing to account for my sudden awakening. I felt absolutely refreshed and couldn't stay in bed. I figured that it would be great for me to use this opportunity and get me some breakfast down at the diner, which I could never do before because I was always asleep.

As my breakfast is brought to me, something that I didn't order is placed beside my breakfast. You guessed it—an orange! Immediately I thought *"Wow!"* but that *Wow* turned into a *"wait a minute, the hand was supposed to bring me the orange at my house."* So, I simply told the waitress *"Oh, I'm sorry, but I didn't order an orange."* *"It's on the house,"* she replied. I thought that maybe her mention of the word *house* fulfilled that part of the manifestation, but I wasn't convinced. I ate, then I left the diner with the orange in hand. On my short walk home I came across a few people I knew in the neighborhood and tried to give them the orange. Nobody would accept it! I get home, unlock the door, and as I step in, my head (for some unknown reason) slowly turns downward to catch sight of my hand slowly lifting (the very hand I had visualized) and holding the orange in the exact *way* I had visualized! I was stunned.

At that very moment I realized that no matter what I may have done, the super-conscious mind was going to produce that orange in precisely the same way that I had presented the image of the orange to it. It reciprocated perfectly. The omnipotent aspect of our subjective mind can always be relied upon for this mutual correspondence. You can ignore and forget that it is there, but you can never turn it off.

By the example above, I wouldn't want you to think that visualization alone is the entirety of the process involved in producing effects in your life. There are several elements that I will discuss individually in detail throughout this book, and then bring them all together for you.

Scrutinizing your list may now have taken on an importance that you probably didn't consider when you first wrote it out.

Human Nature

If there were to remain within you the strong urge to use your newly-found power to get back at someone who may have slighted you in the past, or if you wish to put others in potentially harmful and disadvantageous positions because you don't get along with them or for whatever reason you may have for doing so, I strongly suggest that you turn away from those thoughts. If you prefer for certain people to be out of your life experience because the contribution that they make to your life seems burdensome to you, there is a better way that this can happen without shooting yourself in the foot.

Anything negative or harmful that you may desire originates with your lower-self. This is the part of you that gives its power away, that doesn't believe in the oneness of all, and that does not emanate the qualities of the higher self. The inclination of the lower-self involves the emanation of suboptimal thoughts and emotions. The universal mind will in turn incorporate these emanations in the manifestation that must return to you thru the Reciprocal Circuit. It will bring to you *hatred* if hatred was present when you emitted your signal. If it was *revenge,* you will experience revenge. Plus, the more negativity that is emanated through the Reciprocal Circuit, the more negativity you will have in your life experience. You get what you give.

I mention that there is a better way, and, of course, an omnipotent mind *must* have a better way! You want certain things and circumstances in your life because you believe that if you had them you would be *happier.* In the experience I had with the orange, it became clear to me that the Universal Mind, with its *Infinite Intelligence,* knew exactly what to do, and worked behind the scenes in perfect precision. If you let it know that happiness is what it should "send" to you, it can do so because it already knows what will make you happy. But it won't do so if your desire for happiness is accompanied by an emanation of a current of negativity. Believing that your desire for happiness will be appeased while emanating a vibrational frequency which says "I don't have the happiness I'm asking for" will only give you what you are asking for. *The emanation equals the asking!*

Emanate the signal of present joyfulness, and Infinite Intelligence will turn its wheels to make it a reality in your life. You will see negative elements in your life fade away, whether these are people, their disposition towards you, or particular circumstances. Negativity may have seemed useful and effective as you tried to survive in this physical world, but as you harness the mind's omnipotence, you will be able to easily rise above that illusory belief.

You Already Have It

It can be misleading to say that we "send" intentions to the super-conscious part of the mind. It isn't as if we visualize the super-conscious mind and "put" something in it, nor do we think a thought and let it "fly off" to the Universal Mind. We are only aware of our conscious mind, and we do our mental work with our consciousness. The super-conscious part of the mind operates from a higher level of awareness, but it can only work with the contents that the conscious mind provides. Such contents need to be *compatible* with the higher self in order to manifest what is desired. By *intentionally modifying how we emanate,* we can tap into our super-consciousness and therefore *unlock* the subjective abilities that are inherent within our omnipotent mind.

When we accomplish this, the cooperative work between our consciousness and super-consciousness is automatic, so there is no need to actually "send" anything anywhere—there is *nowhere* to send it *to* because it is all *here* and *now! Maintaining* a specific attitude (not the *sending* of an attitude) is what determines the quality of the current. I will continue, though, to use such terms as *send* and *receive* in order to make the description of the process possible to the extent allowed by the limits of our language.

Keep in mind that what is being described herein operates in a realm beyond the limits of time and space as we know it, and what we perceive as sending and receiving is a more advanced process in this other realm. It operates instantaneously and *precisely*. So, if you think "I am sending this" or "I am sending that," your reality will be a manifested sending. Sending takes time. What you want to do is *have!* You do this by showing the super-conscious mind that you *already have it,* knowing it's already available. Even though it hasn't been manifested yet in consensus reality, you don't focus on that, because it doesn't matter. It will only matter to your lower self. Just *know* that it's a done deal. The super-conscious mind already sees it as a reality before you do. It will only give it to you if you connect with it vibrationally. And the only way that you can connect with it in regards to any particular desired manifestation is if your conscious mind perceives it as an accomplished manifestation— just as it is seen by the super-conscious mind.

This is precisely how the Reciprocal Circuit can be *intentionally* used to bring to you everything you truly desire in life. You may say, "but, if I don't *really* have it, how can I *perceive* that I have it?" In the second part of this book we'll cover that issue thoroughly, but for now *know* that the super-conscious mind does not find a distinction between, let's say, a Ferrari that you actually see with your own eyes and is actually in front of you in your physical presence, and your *mental creation* of the same Ferrari. Don't think, though, that you can fool the intelligence of your omnipotent mind by simply presenting an image to it. If you hold the belief that the image is *merely an image,* the vibrational essence of that very belief will be sent through the circuit, and it will leave the super-conscious mind unconvinced of your vibrational connection to its manifestational reality. You must *authenticate* that you already possess it by genuinely believing that it is a *present* reality. The genuine *belief* will produce a genuine *feeling* of its reality. This also works the other way around: *The genuine feeling will bring about the requisite belief.*

Many people consider this way of thinking to be delusional, and goes way beyond wishful thinking. I've experimented with mere wishful thinking, and I can tell you that as a system for achieving a person's desired results, it falls short of realizing one's desired reality. The reason for this is because the belief and feeling of *already having it* is always missing from mere wishful thinking. We must go beyond such a method. As far as delusional thinking is concerned, well, label it what you will, but as soon as the object of "delusion" makes its appearance as a physical reality for you and everyone else to see, any argument supporting the notion of delusion becomes null and void. This isn't to deny the fact that delusional people may exist among us due to disorders of the mind, but that is a completely separate issue. Such people have no control over their disorders. Our power to intentionally choose what we believe makes all the difference.

Manifesting with Prayer

> *Whatever you desire, when you pray,*
> *believe that you receive them,*
> *and you will have them.*
> —Mark 11:24

Prayer, as a method of obtaining what one desires in life, can be quite effective when certain factors play a role in the prayer itself. Prayers yield a wide range of results in the lives of practically all religious and non-religious practitioners alike. Some feel that most of their prayers are answered, while others find that only a few are answered, still yet a great many continue to wait to see any evidence of an answer.

What accounts for such a disparity in results? Is it due to a person's failure to comply with religious requirements? Is it because some people are more deserving than others? I have found that these are not the reasons. The power that "receives" prayers will respond to each and every one of them according to how they are "sent." Those who feel that they have yet to receive an answer are simply those who do not know how to pray effectively.

Prayer is a *mental* and *emotional* process. It involves the focusing of specific intent which emanates specific vibrational signals. During the emanation of these vibrational frequencies, you must know that the power indeed does *exist* for the fulfillment of your prayer, believe that it is *already* granted, and *feel* the accompanying feelings, such as appreciation and relief, that comes with having received it. The people who fail to see their prayers answered are those that either doubt the *creator's* existence or that the *creator* is even listening; do not believe that it is, will, or can be granted; or simply don't feel the feelings that should accompany such belief. This is mainly due to the fact that the person finds it difficult to remove their focus from their existing condition that they are praying about.

Wrong ways to pray are prayers containing statements such as

"*... if you really exist ...*"
"*... if you are listening ...*"
"*... if you want to ...*"

These are incorrect because the power *does* exist, *and always has;* it is *always* "listening" or receptive; and It's ability to bring forth results has absolutely nothing to do with whether it "wants to," but on your own vibrational offering. The results of ones prayers are based solely on *how* one prays. The process of prayer uses the same Reciprocal Circuit that will do what it does regardless of whether a person attaches a religious connotation to it or not. If it is more meaningful and effective for you to make such an attachment, then by all means do so. If you wish to not call it prayer, then don't. Whatever works for you so long as the elements involved are the ones that actually produce results in your life.

Chapter Three

Time and Change

A very fundamental aspect of everything in existence is *change*. Everything changes! This includes all physical matter everywhere. An object you may have stored in the attic years ago has been undergoing change that cannot be seen with the naked eye. The particles that make up a chair do not stay static in any one particular spot. Even at the quantum level everything is composed of energy which is always moving and spiraling. So it goes with our personal lives, our bodies, relationships, emotions, careers, beliefs, and anything else you can think of. Change is not only *necessary*, it is *inevitable!*

Resistance to Change

Often we are admonished: *You must be willing to accept change.* Why is it so difficult for many to accept change in their lives? For many people, their present level of comfort is indicative of some type of fear, and once something threatens to intrude upon or disrupt their comfort-zone, that fear is revealed. Change can make a person panic, cause stress, sorrow, and for some people it becomes so overwhelming that they go ballistic or even pass out. The perceived random quality of the events that surface in life can bring chaos to many people. This is understandable especially when you consider the fact that living in comfort is very desirable, and that the *periphery* of everyone's comfort-zone can vary drastically from person to person.

The present comfort-zone of a person can be *expanded* to a degree that allows benefits to be obtained which surpass the mere lowering of stress levels. The changeless spirit is like an ocean. When we look at an ocean with its changing waves, can we conceive of the ocean's waves without the ocean itself? Of course not. (If we could, they wouldn't be the *ocean's* waves.) Yet, we *can* conceive of the ocean without its waves. In the same manner, spirit will always exist as the true essence behind our ever-changing reality. It is *that* which causes the appearance and disappearance of these fluctuating waves of manifestation. Source or spirit Itself cannot change or cease to be. That which can change can stop existing because it is a product of the changeless, not the other way around.

Viewing our experiences from the perspective of our unchanging omnipotent mind, the fear of the unknown vanishes.

The world is then a brand new place with every passing moment, and you look forward to each of those moments, come what may. By thus identifying yourself with your causative nature, you can then understand and accept change because *you can effect change yourself,* and you are not without control of what happens in your life. The waves of confusion begin to form coherently in line with purpose.

Overview of Time

The process of change requires the factor of time. The eternal spirit has its beingness outside of the constraints and boundaries of time. Time is a *concept* rather than an actual *thing.* It is a system which we use to measure motion in space. For this process of measurement to occur, there must be a *measurer* or *observer* of the motion, action, or event that occurs in space. That is why Einstein referred to *spacetime* as a continuum of what we are actually experiencing, instead of space and time as independent concepts.

The mystery that accompanies the appearance of randomly changing and unexpected circumstances in life can be a contributing factor to the fear of what life may hold for some people, what destiny may be awaiting them. There are situations in life which appear as if we have absolutely no control over them. These things can be overwhelming if we continue to view them in such a way. But there is another way to stay on top of all events *before* they happen, and even before you become adept at engineering your desired reality.

Before you can begin to be in control of what happens in your life, you must adopt a new way of *viewing* the various changes life presents to you. Consider everything that you have ever experienced in your *past*, connect that time-stream with whatever you are experiencing *now* as you read these words, then connect the present to everything that you will ever experience in the *future* (though it may seem to be out of your view). You should now have *one* long, consecutive stream of events. The events that occurred to you in the past may not have been known to you before they actually happened, nevertheless they *did* eventually happen. It is the same with the future—events *are* going to happen, but your *choices* are what determine how events unfold. The choices that must now take priority, are choices of how you view and feel about everything that you experience and can experience.

Complete Time-Consciousness

Once you are able to consciously handle the seemingly random events that life throws at you, you will be in a better position to remove time's veil of illusion. The concept of time cannot exist without consciousness because all concepts, including that of time, proceed from the mind. Yet, when the mind imprisons itself within temporal measurements and concepts which are incongruous to its native state, it significantly restricts its access to its own inherent potential. The *complete* view of time that is natural to spirit, supports its freedom of ability.

The very view you maintain about the nature of time will either imprison you or allow you to be the master of your destiny. The usual view of time is based on *linear, uni-directional thinking.* When you expand your thinking to *non-linear, multi-directional thinking,* you open up opportunities for change that you never saw before due to the simple fact that...

... you weren't looking for them...

... you weren't looking for them because you didn't believe they existed or that they were possible...

...you didn't believe they were possible because of your limited concept of time... and

... the reason you adopted this limited linear, uni-directional thinking process is because *everyone else around you was using it.*

Non-linear, multi-directional thinking is possible because *the mind is not dependent on time for its own existence.* Once your eyes are opened to the true reach-potential of the mind with regard to time, you will never limit yourself again.

Time is usually viewed as traveling in a straight line into the future. This is the limited view held by most people, and so I call it *incomplete time-consciousness.* To expand our consciousness of time we must begin with what we call *present time.* The present time that we currently experience is not the only present time that exists. It is the one we have consciously or unconsciously chosen to experience. At this very moment, co-existing simultaneously, is an infinite amount of present-time parallel or alternate realities or universes which we haven't chosen. Each one of these has its own particular vibratory quality. The next consecutive moment can be any potential-reality-moment chosen from the infinite possibilities available for that position in time. Choosing what our present time is to consist of involves our ability to *equate what is presently real with a particular vibrational frequency taken from the selection of all potential realities.* Instead of being available linearly, as on a time-track, these possibilities are instantaneously available as if they exist on a perpendicular splay or span on that specific momentary position in time. The same applies to every instant of time.

As expansive as this concept of time may appear, it is still incomplete. The belief that the arrow of time can only point and "move forward" into the future is another concept which has taken away your power to alter your reality. Time only *appears* to move forward. Any point in time is instantaneously accessible to you in order to see it and/or alter it. To speak of a past, present, and future is to lock yourself into the linear view of time, whereas the past and future do not exist in the same manner that the present exists. Everything we can ever know of what is called past and future is only *knowable in the present* because that is the only place you can access them from.

Since we do have access to the past and future in the present, whatever is in the past cannot be a finished, irreversible product; and whatever is in the future is neither unforeseeable nor immalleable—unless we *decide* that they are. These time references are not far-away, unreachable places. They are here and now within our grasp. The concept of your ability to modify the past or future as needed, will be much easier to understand when you realize that every moment of the past and future have their own infinite possible realities existing simultaneously, and that these are also within the reach of your consciousness in Present-Time.

Chapter Four

Energy and Conscious Intention

Quantum science has produced sufficient evidence indicating that the *law of mind* exists and that we are *observer-participants* in the universe. What this basically means is that we cannot observe, or be *aware* of something in our known universe without *influencing* it. Our consciousness, in this context, is postulated as being able to perceive *objectively* what we have created *subjectively*.

The following is a concise overview of significant discoveries made in this field, and how it relates to mind power.

Quantum Proof of Mind Power

The double-slit experiment, where it all began, is the well-known scientific experiment which was conducted in 1801 for the first time by Thomas Young. As the experiment was repeated by other scientists in subsequent years it continued to show that quantum energy, such as the photon, can display the properties of a particle or the properties of a wave, but not both simultaneously. It can change from one to the other. This was the discovery of *wave-particle duality*. Yet, not until 1924 were the waves postulated as being *probability waves* by Bohr, Kramers, and Slater. This means that when it is a particle, it is in a *defined* state, but as a wave it is in a state of *potentiality*, a state of *infinite possibilities* termed the "wave function." Then the hypothesis of *Schrodinger's Cat* posed by Erwin Schrodinger, illustrated that the single factor which determined and chose the actual outcome out of all probabilities represented by a particular wave, was *the observer's very observation of the experiment itself.* Then in 1927 Niels Bohr's *Principle of Complementarity* explained that not only does the phenomena of wave-particle duality exist because of the observer, but that the *choosing* from all existing probabilities occurs because the observer is actually *interacting* with the quantum energy. Again in 1927, the Copenhagen Interpretation of Quantum Mechanics agreed with the notion that the reason we *perceive* objective reality is because we are subjectively *constructing* it.

We are Creating our Reality!

When we are in the process of observing, we are also in the process of interpreting, expecting, defining, and believing certain things *about* what we are observing. These subjective processes *determine* how the object of observation will be influenced during the interaction. That makes us more as participants than as mere observers. In scientific terms, when we are observing, we are also "taking a measurement." Therefore, in this context, an observation *is* a measurement. In 1957 the Everett-Wheeler-Graham theory (better known as the *Many Worlds Interpretation* of Quantum Mechanics) stated that all of the possibilities represented by the wave, end up actually occurring in their own worlds which exist simultaneously with our own, yet we are only aware of, and experience the actualization of, one of those possibilities in our own world. The conclusion drawn from these discoveries is that consciousness—the very activity of spirit—influences the behavior of matter and of reality.

Are ultra-sensitive, high-tech equipment needed to observe a particle in order to influence its behavior? In 1924, Louis de Broglie had theorized what was later proven through experimentation, starting with the Davisson-Germer experiment: No only does the wave-particle duality exist at the sub-atomic level, but it also exists at the atomic and molecular level, what we *normally* understand as matter. Then in 1964, *Bell's Theorem* which was published by J.S. Bell, stated that separate parts in the universe do not exist as such, but that *everything has a connection not only at a micro level, but at a macro level as well.* Since everything that exists in the micro- and macrocosm are connected and possess a wave-particle duality, consciousness can potentially influence whatever it observes, along with anything it cannot observe, but which must necessarily be affected indirectly by virtue of its connection with what is being observed directly.

How is it possible for our subjective consciousness to interact with external reality by the process of observing it? The interaction between mind and matter occurs via a medium called *subtle energy force* that our machines have yet to record. It was fascinating enough when not long ago Dr. Vladimir Poponin discovered the DNA Phantom Effect which recorded the influential effects that DNA molecules have on quantum particles, which effect could only be possible with the existence of a force that defines subtle energy, but more impressive was when Dr. Glen Rein also conducted recent experiments which show that we influence our DNA *subjectively and at a distance*, with nothing to account for such influence but for the hidden factor of subtle energy. That the influence of this force is of a non-local nature and is unaffected by the constraints of time, has also been proven by Clive Backster who began conducting his own experiments in 1966.

Up to now, all that can be seen are the effects of this mysterious medium, just as we can only detect the effect of gravity between things that have mass. The existence of the hypothetical graviton particle itself has yet to be discovered using the equipment available to us. That is because gravity is nothing other than a degree or expression of the same subtle energy force that pervades the entire universe, and which allows an influential connection to exist between the mind and the material world. Therefore, if we can influence one particle, what is there to prevent us from influencing many, any, and all particles?

The existence of Infinite Possibilities has always been with us. Our reality has the potential to be changed to anything we decide it to be. The implications of this are astounding considering the fact that current mainstream beliefs about the nature of reality need no longer be forced upon us if we don't want them to be. We can make use of this "new" discovery and choose to engineer our own reality.

Subtle Energy Force

Many further scientific experiments have been conducted involving the role that consciousness plays in the manipulation of the energy that our material universe is composed of. I provide some examples of consciousness experiments to show that the omnipotent mind is no mere fantasy or idea without a scientific basis. Their results will encourage you to rethink much of what you thought you knew about the relationship between the mind and the world around us.

The DNA Phantom Effect is a phenomenon that was discovered relatively recently by Dr. Vladimir Poponin. He found that, just as Kirlian photography has captured the phantom fields of leaves and human limbs that have been severed from their main bodies, revealing the same shape of the missing part, so does DNA leave evidence of such a field. He reports that the DNA phantom field has an "intrinsic ability to couple with conventional electromagnetic fields" allowing a sophisticated spectrometer to display this effect on his monitor. The experiment began with quantum particles that were contained within a vacuum tube. These particles went from what was an initial unorganized state to an orderly one when human DNA was introduced into the tube. Even more remarkable was the fact that the particles continued to remain influenced by the human DNA sample *after* the DNA sample was removed from the tube. It left behind an orderly-shaped spiral that coincided exactly with the DNA's helix. Later experiments confirmed that the *subsequent behavior* of the particles was directly related to the *subsequent manipulation* of the withdrawn DNA molecule. In other words, the behavior occurred at the same time that the manipulation was occurring.

What this shows us is that an invisible, organizing influence exists between our DNA and quantum particles which allows for an interaction to occur even from a distance. This connective energy is *subtle energy,* which is also the invisible carrier of our intentions.

The presence of this energy, though, is not limited to DNA. It is present with everything that exists; in fact, it is *because* of this connective energy's role as carrier of our intentions that we influence things around us every day in ways in which we are completely unaware of. For example, in 1966 Clive Backster, one of the most renowned experts of the polygraph machine, decided one day out of boredom and curiosity, to apply the electrodes of his machine to the leaf of a tropical plant he had in his office. The readouts were unmistakable. He could clearly see that his thoughts, intentions, and emotions were instantaneously received by the plant.

In one instance, when Backster had the machine hooked up to the plant, he had the thought to light a match in order to burn one of its leaves and see what would happen. The very moment the thought had occurred to him to do this, the needle on the machine began indicating that the plant was in extreme distress just as a human being would react! Later, if Backster simply *pretended* to attempt to burn the leaf, there was no reaction from the plant, as if the plant picked up the distinction of a *faked* intention.

Further experiments with plants revealed that the presence of positive emotions would make plants thrive, whereas in the presence of negative emotions they would eventually wither and not fare well at all, no matter how well they were taken care of otherwise.

Experiments conducted by Masaru Emoto have also indicated that even water molecules are significantly affected by our thoughts and emotions.

The Intention Experiment, an ongoing series of experiments being led by Lynne McTaggart, is showing the powerful effects that occur when thousands of participants from around the world direct their intention with the same goal in mind.

These experiments merely provide a glimpse of the potential that our properly-directed thoughts have due to the existence of the ever-present subtle energy force.

* * *

In 1998 I personally began a daily yogic meditative practice of sitting and observing. With my eyes closed I just observed my breathing, my body, and allowed any intruding stream of thought to "float by." In that year I had several significant experiences during these sessions, but more to the point of our discussion is what occurred one day when I was *not* in a meditative state.

I met up with a friend of mine as I regularly did each week, and as we reached out to shake hands, several inches before his hand even touched mine, he pulled his hand back abruptly and said *"Whoa! What the hell was that?!"* From afar he suspiciously inspected the inside of my hand as if I was concealing something. Bewildered by his behavior, I asked *"What?"* He responded by asking *"Didn't you feel that?"* *"Feel what?"* I asked. Assured that I had nothing in my hand he reached out again more slowly and carefully with his hand until our palms were parallel with each other and about five to six inches apart. Again, *"Whoa!"* he excitedly pulls back his hand, massaging it with his other hand. This time he had a big smile on his face and said *"Oh my God, how'd you do that?"* Not having felt what he felt, I said *"I didn't even touch you."* *"Yeah, I know,"* he said, *"but I felt a sort of a strong shock, yet it was more of a pleasant electric tingling which connected our hands! How could you not feel that?"*

I carefully watched his expression for any indication that he was just being humorous. He was not. Whatever he felt left a lasting impression on him, convincing me of the genuineness of his experience. I immediately associated my friend's experience with my meditative practice, which is akin to the first few exercises found in this book. The question that remained with me was why hadn't I felt anything whereas my friend did? There was an obvious phenomenon occurring between us due to the proximity of both our hands, yet I felt nothing at all.

The answer to the above question became easy for me to understand as I continued my meditations. These meditations allowed me to be more attuned or sensitive to an energy which has access to high vibrational frequencies that I was not aware of beforehand. My body apparently began to align itself to the magnification of this energy which remained with me even after my sessions. The energy that emitted from my hand had an immediate effect on the lower vibration emitted by my friend's hand, thereby having an uplifting effect that he could actually feel. The hands are one of the areas of the human body that an exchange of energy can occur in a highly concentrated form. This particular energy, subtle energy, is a sort of *mental sense of touch,* and a carrier of varying vibrational frequencies. It cannot itself be felt, but you can feel its transformative effects which occur when other fine vibrational patterns interact by means of it. The reason I felt nothing at that moment was because the transformative effects were not occurring to me at that particular moment, but to my friend. This does not mean that I can't allow myself to feel effects that subtle energy can cause. It all depends on the intention. Little did I know that this energy was an instrument that allowed for miraculous things to occur.

Archaically referred to as *etheric force*, and more recently called *tachyon* or *torsion energy*, subtle energy force continues to elude direct scientific measurement due to its ultra-invisible nature. This also appears to be what Dr. William Tiller labels as *deltrons*, which act as a conduit allowing our conscious intentions to reach the vacuum which underlies normal reality in order to bring changes in the latter.

David Sereda has also noted that from this vacuum, energy/mass (or manifestations) can be *pulled* from higher dimensions into our universe when torsion fields are created.

A quantum scientist observing his or her experiments can see what is actually happening with the assistance of highly-calibrated state-of-the-art machinery. What the scientist doesn't see is what lies beneath—the subtle energy which is the medium that makes it all possible. This is the logistical link between the conscious mind and the external world. Subtle energy is the carrier we use to reach the super-conscious mind in order to make our mental creations a reality. Our emotions, beliefs, and whatever we create with our imaginative powers, are carried by this energy into the vacuum of super-consciousness. The application of well-directed intention, allows us to become aware of the degree that the intensity of subtle energy flow is magnified for the purpose of manifesting what we desire. *Once our perception of it is amplified by means of our feeling and emotions, it will act as a conduit through which our beliefs and intentions travel in order for our omnipotent mind to receive them and make them a reality.*

Subtle energy is very fine and its frequency is one that is much higher and finer than the frequency of the photon. Such a high frequency is the blueprint of the conduit called the Reciprocal Circuit. It allows for access to dimensional levels that the photon we know of cannot reach. This is because the speed limit restricted to our physical dimension cannot exceed the photon's speed of light. When it does exceed that speed, it fails to remain in our physical dimension.

Thus, subtle energy is superluminal, existing beyond the influences of spacetime restraints, which is where ordinary consciousness also exists. Consciousness can sense the activity of subtle energy by means of the body, especially through the skin, and particularly through our hands and the *heart* region of our bodies, which is the seat of our emotions. This region is situated along the core of our energetic field called the *sushumna,* a central channel of highly-concentrated subtle energy extending from the base of the perineum, up through all of our main energy centers (which includes the Heart center), and up through the top of the head. It is about three to four inches in diameter as it rises, and narrows as it goes through the throat area. It is always active, rotating in one direction or the other, emanating its invisible force in all directions. The speed of rotation and degree of emanation coincides directly with the degree of intensity of our feelings and emotions. This intensity is magnified through *conscious breathing,* which is part of the reason that in many meditative practices we are taught to "watch the breath." Breathing is an integral part of our emotions, whether they be sorrow, fear, anger, or exhilaration. We breathe more when we feel more, and we also feel more when we breathe more.

When we are watching, or observing, the very act of observing involves a connection between the observer and the observed. This connection can be initiated by seeing with our physical or our *mental* eyes, and with the sense of feeling induced externally or mentally. When we observe something without judgment, uninfluenced by bias or expectation, but in an objective manner, we automatically allow for the controlled participation of subtle energy to contact that which is observed, and influence it according to the intentions which we have formulated subjectively with our consciously-directed feelings and beliefs.

The practice of magnifying the intensity of subtle energy flow when inducing specific emotions and beliefs, is the most effective way to convince the super-conscious mind to produce the effects we desire to have. The stronger we sense this energy, the more readily manifested our thoughts become. As a matter of fact, we feel subtle energy working all the time, most people just don't recognize it as such, and neither do they intentionally attempt to increase their sensitivity of the vibrational frequencies that travel through it. They just go through life believing that external events make them feel whatever they feel, that they have no conscious choice but to be an effect. Only a relatively few come to realize that they can fully influence their inner world, and cause themselves to feel whatever they want to feel at will. Additionally, you can engineer your reality with the use of *conscious breathing, the power of your imagination, awareness,* and *choice of meaning (intention)*. You can combine these elements with your *power of belief* and thereby produce what you had previously thought was impossible.

Becoming Aware of Subtle Energy

You can feel this fine energy-force working right now if you wanted to. It's just a matter of becoming aware of it. Inducing sensitivity to it in your body is quite easy, and gets easier with practice. Follow these simple steps to acquaint yourself with the sensation that accompanies this energy:

Exercise Two

1. Sit or lie down in a quiet place, close your eyes and relax your entire body. Just let go of any physical tenseness.

2. Become aware of your breath and maintain this awareness throughout, as if you were independently observing your breathing from a distance.

3. Allow yourself to breathe regularly and a little more deeply than normal.

4. As you continue to do this, become aware of your entire body. Look at it from within, as a whole unit.

5. Completely still and relaxed, become as sensitive as you can to your entire skin surface. Allow your skin to feel as much as possible the air that is in contact with it, sensing it very distinctly with extreme focus of your attention. *(Focusing attention does not require tensing up).*

6. Increase this sensation as much as you can and hold it as long as you can, maintaining the breathing pattern. Heightening the sensation intensifies the power of the subtle energy which accompanies it. If your grip on the sensation diminishes, bring it back up again. This usually means that your attention has strayed from your skin to some other thought.

The overall feeling this exercise may have left you with is similar to what you feel after moments of heightened emotion. This is why your breathing is so integral to this process. Varying your breathing will modify the degree of sensitivity you have to this energy, and the more sensitive you are to it the more effective your creative powers become.

The Non-Local Nature of the Mind

The reason it doesn't matter how far away your object of influence may be is because the super-conscious mind operates within a non-local framework instantaneously. To this aspect of the mind there's no difference between a thousand miles and a millimeter. Once an intention is dispatched, it is already there. If your intention is meant for two places that are miles apart in order to fulfill the object of your intention, then they both are reached simultaneously. As you learned in an earlier chapter, the super-conscious mind is above space and time. It uses the subtle energy that exists everywhere to produce anything at any time and any place. Information travels on subtle energy faster than the speed of light because physical light is of a denser, and therefore slower, vibration. In fact, the information doesn't really travel at all—it *is* there once the intention is made.

Vehicles, sound, and light all take time to travel from one location to another because they are all subject to the physical laws of space and time. But, since the mind functions beyond space and time, it is non-local, and therefore needs no time to reach anywhere. Non-locality works like an infinite web that attaches everything to everything else, and allows for communications to occur unimpeded by anything in our known universe, including distance and time.

There are many documented accounts of people experiencing such non-locality in their very lives, as in the cases of mothers knowing exactly when their child was in distress at moments when the child was nowhere near the mother. When investigated afterwards, the mothers would find out that the child was in some type of emotionally-charged situation at the very instant that the mother sensed it.

Additional experiments by Clive Backster also show that distance was not a factor when the plants he had attached to his lie detector demonstrated a synchronized reaction of emotional change whenever the plant's owner, who was on a plane trip far away from the plants, felt the uneasiness that comes with the taking-off and landing of the plane. Using synchronized watches, the reactions were seen to occur at exactly the same time. This also revealed the invisible bond that existed between Backster and his plants.

We're all aware of the bond that exists between mother and child, but can a similar connection exist between other things in our universe (besides plants), establishing a strong enough connection to be able to influence them from miles away? Yes, and we can deliberately induce such a connection to whatever we want by using the power of the mind. Don't limit this connection to things that you have had an intimate relationship with. The mind can create the requisite connection. For instance, create a mental picture of the Great Pyramid. Get up close to it and feel it, look at it from different angles as if you were really there walking around it. Enjoy what you're experiencing, and feel it as a familiar place, as if you've known it all your life, and appreciate that fact. If you have done this properly, then, to a certain degree, you have connected with the *actual* Great Pyramid of Giza located in Egypt! The more vivid and tangible you make the mental picture, the stronger the connection.

What can be *done* with these types of connections depends on how *real* the connection is made. Thoroughly believing in the connection *will* establish the connection and interaction, but thoroughly believing in your ability to *influence* what you're connecting with is further required in order to alter reality. If you were actually in the presence of the Pyramid (which anyone will agree is physically possible), *what interaction do you believe you could have with it that would have an altering influence on its reality?* For an altering influence to occur, you must cross the boundaries of what you believe to be possible. I will show you how to create a very strong bond that will open the door for you to influence anything with the use of the mind, no matter how far away you may be from it! Distance is not a factor with your omnipotent mind.

Heart Meditation

The Heart Meditation Process
is Essential for Manifestation Work

If you want to become the creator of your own reality, but you tend to have a short attention span and are easily distracted, then you must make this section your own.

In order to influence the super-conscious mind effectively, the reality that you desire must be *mentally and emotionally maintained until it dominates as a truth to you.* When it becomes a truth to you, then will the vibrational signals that emanate from the subjective truth that you have created, resonate with the same vibrational truth held by the super-conscious mind—It will then produce the manifestation of that truth for you. If distractions or interruptions of any sort break the maintenance of your desire before it becomes true to you, your vibrational seeds of thought will have fallen on infertile ground. The circuit will not reach completion.

The above not only requires that you learn how to observe, but that you learn how to *maintain an unadulterated and uninterrupted observation of your intended reality until you have attained certainty of its belief.* You must first become master of your *attention* before you can become master of your *reality.* Instead of your attention being pulled here and there, take back this power and develop the ability to direct your attention on what *you* decide, without allowing for any intruding distractions which have nothing to do with what you're aiming for, or even worse, which contradict what you're aiming for.

Additionally, any awareness-development system—such as the Heart Meditation below—must have its foundation in core qualities of the super-conscious mind if it is to manifest what we desire in accordance with the Law of Attraction. This is accomplished with Heart Meditation. You must persist in the proper attentiveness until your goal is achieved. Your goal is achieved when your desire has become *genuinely true to you regardless of outward appearances.* All concepts found in this book will be so much easier for you to effectively apply if this ability to focus and concentrate is developed.

To begin with, a regular practice of the Heart Meditation will play a significant role in clearing away those obstacles that prevent your effective use of the Reciprocal Circuit. A lot has been written about the meditation process. I'll give you the essential nuts-and-bolts, mapping out for you the exact process involved.

You should set aside a regular time for meditation, and it should be done *at least* once a day, but twice would be significantly more beneficial.

Keep a log of your sessions, noting the date, length of time, and any progress you have made.

Exercise Three — The Heart Meditation Process

1. Sit upright in a chair, neither slouched nor tense, but *comfortably set* with your spine straight, hands on your thighs, and feet flat on the floor.

2. Turn your eyes upward at about a *fourty-five-degree* angle. Close your eyes, and then turn them all the way to the right until they won't go anymore. Then turn them all the way to the left in the same fashion. Continue to do this back and forth motion with your eyes, picking up speed until you are at your fastest—always making sure that your eyeballs, still at a fourty-five-degree angle, reach the furthest corners on the right and left. Do this for *two minutes*.

   [You may feel some pressure when you first start to practice this warm-up exercise, but it is partially due to the fact that you are stimulating both hemispheres of your brain, establishing a free flowing of communication between them, and which helps to balance their activity in an optimal way. This balance is a great preparation for the meditation process. The pressure

you feel subsides as you continue with subsequent meditation sessions.]

3. With eyes still closed, breathe evenly and comfortably, releasing any undue tension beginning from the top of your head and going down your body toward your toes.

4. Observe

The only thing you do subjectively is observe the breath and the entire body *in a detached manner* . . . and you continue to observe. The more you are aware of the body by *observing* it, the more you are actually *feeling* it. Let your mind refrain from participating or being affected in any way by anything occurring either inside or outside of the body. Your main goal is to be a completely unaffected observer. The mind should think of nothing in particular. You, as spirit, begin with *the intention to look,* then you do just that.

[Normally, allowing your attention to be pulled by distractions, evinces the power they have over you. That is not true meditation. During the Heart Meditation process, you will notice that numerous unsolicited sensations surface in the body, and that brief images, sounds, memories, and intruding thoughts prod you to become involved, to evaluate, judge or become emotionally affected. All of these things occur exterior to the real You, and your attention on the false power of their unrelenting grip must be re-directed to your true position of power before you can successfully engage yourself in Reality Engineering. Therefore, as you meditate, allow these things to just happen around your awareness until they fade away or at least become very distant. The longer you can do this, the better. These events may intensify before they fade, but eventually they will fade—that is when you have entered true meditation.]

When you are able to achieve the above, then the actual Heart Meditation should begin at this point as follows:

5. Allow your breathing to become *deeper,* while keeping it at a comfortable pace.

6. As you breathe *inward,* feel as if the breath is not only coming in through your nose, but from all directions as you feel it go right to the center of your Heart.

7. As you feel the breath coming in, feel it as *having* the most beautiful quality of unconditional love or any other uplifting quality that is easy for you to feel.

8. Simultaneously, feel appreciation *for* the breath while it is coming in and reaching your Heart center.

9. When you breathe outward, let the breath assume the same path as when it came in, while continuing the same feelings that this Heart Meditation calls for.

10. Let the feelings of appreciation, beauty, and unconditional love build higher and higher with each incoming and outgoing breath.

11. Continue the Heart Meditation for *at least fifteen minutes.*

12. The Silence

    If the Heart Meditation is done properly, you will reach the state of *Pure Observer* where all of the "noise" and subjective interruptions have disappeared. *This is true meditation.* You have now entered a silent waiting period where you may notice various phenomena which are very distinct from the previous distractions. You may feel extremely light and serene, or situated in the center of your body or head while your body feels gigantic as if you, as spirit, were a star within the universe of the body. You may even find yourself outside of your body. You are safe and in a position of power, so remain at ease. By continuing to maintain your position as observer in this waiting period, you will eventually enter . . .

13. Divine Consciousness

By allowing no interruption during the waiting period, higher levels of consciousness will eventually open up to you. During meditation, when you reach the natural state of spirit, which is beyond space and time, a brilliant light, the sense of *all-knowing, all-loving, all-joy, unity with all, and infinite peace* may engulf you. Many describe this experience as *spiritual enlightenment.*

[It is also possible to experience what is referred to as kriya movements. These are movements and/or positions of the body that seem to run on their own. They will vary from person to person, sometimes resembling yoga positions, traditional Indian dances, mudra positions, etc. Specific movements are actually selected, induced, and guided by the Infinite Intelligence that is your higher self for the purpose of helping you bridge your connection to Source more thoroughly. Whatever you need at the moment in order to help safely accomplish this will be provided.]

After the Heart Meditation Session:
How You Know True Meditation has Occurred

14. Returning to Normal Consciousness

You will notice that when you return to normal consciousness, it may be difficult for you to put into words many of the things that you experienced in that state. All of a sudden the spoken language seems to be deficient in describing the Absolute.

* * *

You may or may not experience the above in your first session, but there will definitely be an unfolding of layers of resistance that may not be readily apparent to you. When you begin noticing the layers come down, they will serve as definite indicators that you are reaping benefit from the practice. You will know that this is happening both *during the meditation process* and *as you tend to your daily affairs.*

Every Heart Meditation session counts. Daily diligence in your practice is so important because you are sharpening a subjective ability that you utilize daily—*the ability to direct your awareness, then maintain your attention on what you've become aware of.* The things that your mind tends to cling to with no letup are innumerable. The clinging is the result of resistance that originates from the lower self. In such a way has your awareness been held hostage or imprisoned in the "normal" human consciousness of your lower self. But you will notice that, as you begin to regularly meditate, the hold that the false self may have had on you will be significantly loosened. Allow yourself to let it go without judgment or any sense of attachment. The time it takes for this to occur differs widely from person to person. Commit yourself to accomplishing this and you will lay a firm foundation for the rest of the exercises and concepts found in this book.

Important: Do not neglect the heart meditation process, it is the practical foundation you need to establish in order to access your omnipotent mind!

Restructuring Patterns of Energy

Erwin Schrodinger had also explained that the particles which make up our material universe aren't particles at all, but are *patterns* which consist of standing waves. These standing wave patterns are what give matter its apparent form. What's important to remember is that characteristic to any wave is its susceptibility of being interfered with by means of interaction. This interaction will cause the "particle" to change its standing wave pattern. The result is a different standing wave pattern with a changed apparent form. When we interact with any apparent form, we interfere with its original wave pattern, its original "structure".

Since all "structures" in the material universe consist of precise energy patterns, and since energy follows thought, any pattern of energy can be reshaped to conform to our own thought patterns when both patterns interact through the medium of subtle energy force. If you have a "bad" knee, then the energy that makes up that knee is presenting itself to you in a disordered state. This distorted pattern (the currently existing standing wave pattern) can be realigned to a perfected and orderly state (changed apparent form), making any pain or injury vanish from the knee.

Notable examples of this are the "presence" healings that were done by Nizier-Anthelme Philippe of Lyons (1849-1905). In one of his sessions a very large woman was picked for him to "treat." The woman suffered from edema, leaving her entire body extremely swollen where it appeared as if she were about to burst. In the presence of the doctors who had inspected the condition of the woman, Philippe stood before the woman whose clothes had suddenly dropped to the floor as she stood there naked and *thin*. The only sign that she ever suffered from her previous condition was the size of the clothes which lay piled around her ankles.

A very impressive experiment highlighting the process of *energy pattern restructuring* involved the use of a raspberry plant. V. Budakovski, a Russian scientist, conducted an experiment in the year 2000 where, using laser technology, he placed the hologram of healthy raspberry tissue inside a sickened raspberry which was all callused. The sick raspberry began healing itself by resonating with the information and vibrational pattern that the hologram provided. Whatever disease the plant may have had was out-pictured (out-*patterned*) by the perfection of the hologram, and eventually the raspberry was completely healed.

Were we to mentally superimpose a person's true natural state of perfection over their diseased appearance in order to out-pattern it, their condition would become re-calibrated back to health as was the raspberry. Our mental construct would interact with the patterns that are holding the person's disease in place, and it would alter them accordingly. The holographic images that the mind can produce are infinitely more powerful than laser holograms. The exercises in this book, such as the creation of thought-forms in real-time, and seeing perfection, will teach you to accomplish this with ease.

The omnipotent mind can do this with anything at all, including everything on your list! The beauty of it is that your task is not to sort out each and every particle of energy in order to get accurate results. Whatever goes on behind the scenes is in the hands of *divine intelligence* which can replace any pattern of energy with any other, and can do so instantaneously! Since you can rely on this process, you need not concern yourself about the mechanics involved therein as Schrodinger did. Knowing *about* the process helps you understand why you must do your part in the conscious world. The super-conscious mind will do the rest automatically.

Everything Vibrates

The reason our thoughts and emotions are so effective in making these transformations is due to the fact that everything consists of vibrational frequencies that influence each other whenever they interact. Vibrations of higher and finer frequencies have transformative effects on denser vibrations. So there exists a hierarchy of vibrations in which the higher vibrations can easily change the lower ones. Our imaginative, thought, belief, and emotional faculties have a desirable molding effect on our reality when properly directed.

All of this is possible because all things that exist have one common Source and origin accessible through the omnipotent mind. Looking at our universe from this viewpoint, we can see that the entire cosmos is a colossal thought—a highly condensed thought. The vibration of matter is much slower than pure thought, but they are basically made of the same "stuff." The connection that exists between one thing and another may not be readily apparent *until we place our awareness on that connection.* And that connection is made possible through the medium of subtle energy. This awareness will affect the vibratory rate of both of those things.

Everything, therefore, emits its own particular vibration, and our consciousness can *equate* any vibrational pattern that is desired. When your thoughts, emotions and beliefs match the vibratory rate of the reality you want, you have essentially eliminated all of the resistance factors that were keeping it away from you to begin with. These vibrations are what constitute the current which you send down the *Reciprocal Circuit.* The super-conscious mind will now be prompted to confirm your belief that it *is* there, by producing it for you. Just as two equally calibrated tuning forks will vibrate simultaneously even though only one of them has been struck, a thought equating the vibrations of a conceived reality, will resonate with the creative ability of super-consciousness, and vibrate that conception into the world of manifestation.

Connecting yourself mentally and emotionally with people and things that you always considered separate from yourself, will change the vibrational frequency of both you and the other until both frequencies approximate each other much more closely than before. This act of connecting is basically what love is. It emanates and can expand from our *heart* region. Love is an extremely high vibration and has the ability to change things very rapidly. *Unconditional love* is unbending and far superior in strength to all other vibrations. Few are those that can sincerely maintain such a love for all of creation at all times. But, it is necessary to acquire the ability to love unconditionally in order for you to make positive changes occur in your life.

You can also become aware of the vibrations of your environment, not just the vibrations in your body. Therefore, you can expand this awareness to include your immediate surroundings, allowing positive emotions such as appreciation, acceptance, and love to be absorbed all around you. Your only limitation as to how far you can expand this awareness, is your belief in that limitation. You must be prepared to let go of any limiting beliefs that may present itself, and which may be preventing your attunement with this divine expression.

You don't have to actually focus on subtle energy itself, because the moment you are aware of your surroundings and feel love, the subtle energy is *already there* doing its job automatically by connecting your love vibrations to the environmental vibrations. These will interact, and an influence will occur thereby. Emotions can vary in intensity, and the environmental vibrational patterns will adjust to the degree that your love is amplified. Intense emotional vibrations will attract things of similar vibrations, as well as repel those that are not.

Calibrating vibrations to equate specific vibrations of a past thing or event will have the effect of connecting to it in order to influence it from the present. If all events, including those in the past, proceed from, and are always available to the mind, then it is only the mind that would either allow or prevent the making of any changes in the past that we would like to make. This also applies to future events. Very real and tangible effects can be produced this way, not just the mere altering of past memories and future expectations.

PART TWO

REALITY ENGINEERING

Chapter Five

Choosing New Realities

The Power of Choice

One of the abilities that we as sentient beings tend to underestimate and take for granted is the ability of the mind to *choose*. Many people strongly believe that their choices can be limited or taken away. It is common to hear *"I had no other choice!"* Whenever you hear yourself say those words, recognize it as a sign of limited thinking. The power of choice is the bedrock of *unlimited power*. Your ability to choose anything at any time is staring you right in the face. The universe is practically crying out for you to do so. By choosing what to think, what to believe, and what to feel, you are able to manifest your desired reality out of the infinite possibilities that are always available. Whether or not you are *willing* to make particular choices under particular circumstances is another matter. This may be due to a fear or resistance to *change,* of the uncertainty that comes when one ventures *beyond their familiar comfort-zone* as was discussed earlier. The power rests with you, don't give it away to illusory sources of power.

You always have a choice, and your choices are very powerful. When your range of decisions is small, it is because you may also have bought into the belief of "unavailable options." This is a self-imposed mental prison suggested by others who had already espoused that very belief. Total freedom of choice is a basic quality of the spirit that can never be taken away.

Werner Heisenberg's *Uncertainty Principle* explains that *reality* cannot exist separately from *consciousness* and its ability to *choose*, because reality always presents to an observer choices in the form of *reciprocals* (also called *conjugate variables*). A reciprocal is like a toggle-switch (as an on/off switch). The switch itself is only *one* switch or lever with *two* extreme options. If the operator of the switch chooses the extreme option of *off*, then the operator can only observe or experience *off*, it cannot observe or experience *on* to any degree, much less its extreme. In other words, both extreme options cannot be observed or experienced *simultaneously*. The fact that we experience reciprocals in this way is proof that the actual power to choose what one wishes to observe, rests only with the observer, the switch operator.

This *switch* exists intrinsically within consciousness. By choosing to completely observe, measure, determine, or believe something about one of two reciprocals, we automatically exclude any experience of the other reciprocal, and vice versa. Try this yourself. The extreme of reciprocals are like two sides of the same coin. Hold a coin in front of one eye, and close your other eye. Now try to see if you can directly observe with your one eye the two surfaces of the coin *at the same time*. You will find that you cannot. What you can do is choose to observe only one side at a time, and every choice automatically and invariably excludes the view of the other side of the coin. Yet, the two choices you can choose from come from the same one coin. That is how reciprocals work.

The important point to note here is that not only are these options *available*, but they are available only to consciousness because these options *belong* only to consciousness. It only *appears* that the universe is granting us these options, when in fact it is showing that we are the ones in control of the granting of (and the choosing from) these options as observer/participants. The choices wouldn't exist if there were no observer to *see* that they exist and consequently *choose* from between them. In other words, *we choose how to see and determine reality.*

Making a choice is a subjective process, and in order to achieve the results that we are talking about, choice-making must become a more dynamic process than what you're normally used to. In order to determine reality, in order for something to become or *be real*, the choice to determine its realness cannot be an incomplete choice or determination. Our attention cannot be divided between two inversely related reciprocals. The switch must either be fully *on* or fully *off* with regard to the choices with which we decide to engineer our reality. For our purposes the most important reciprocals that exist are *Time* and *Energy* which are easily illustrated using the model of the *Black Hole Phenomenon*.

The Black Hole Phenomenon

The fastest speed that can be measured in the universe is the speed of light. This measurement is possible because light exists in time. The speed and motion of subtle energy, on the other hand, cannot be measured because it has neither speed nor motion, exists outside of time, and is therefore invisible. This brings us to the phenomenon of the black hole which exhibits a gravitational pull so powerful and so complete that nothing in the universe, not even light itself, can escape it.

Once through the hole, where does everything go? Another universe, or better said, another reality. At the very threshold of the hole, which is invisible (because gravity is invisible), time and space (called *spacetime* because they both are part of an inseparable continuum) have become infinitely warped to the point that time stands completely still, and *all* space curves into itself to become *no* space. Spacetime essentially would not exist anymore, and it is at that exact point that anything that has been grasped by the full attraction of this gravitational force can be assigned a different reality because the laws of physics of "normal reality" have been *suspended.* This is so because the more energy the black hole has, the more entropy (disorder, a suspension or lack of law) it has. [For all of you theoretical physicists out there, it is *within* this invisible suspension that Heisenberg's *Uncertainty Principle* also ceases to exist].

Outside of this hole, everything exists in time, and things are what they're expected to be in terms of obeying the laws of physics. The hole itself, though, does not contain the factor of time nor space, allowing for all possibilities to be simultaneously and immediately available at that point. That is why passage to the other side is passage to another reality. Ordinary reality *needs* time in order to keep things as they are, and to make unavailable any other options that are beyond the *status quo.*

What significance does this have to Reality Engineering? Whether or not scientists have actually found black holes in outer space, or many tiny ones all around us, the theory describing a black hole happens to also describe subtle energy force. Time and Energy are two reciprocals on the same *switch.* Shut off time (spacetime) completely and you experience the absolute energy needed to unlock omnipotence. Unlimited *access* to subtle energy allows for unlimited *options* to be available due to the removal of the limiting factors of time and space. Becoming completely aware of energy through *what we feel* is the same as throwing the *switch* to *energy,* thereby allowing our subjective power of choice to be fully effective in the invisible realm of super-consciousness. It is our level of belief that heightens our ability to feel enough energy in order to do this. This very concept of the power that black holes have, is what our own mind is capable of by the use of subtle energy force.

Until one learns to do this in a complete sense, they are like a dimmer switch sometimes achieving incomplete or mediocre results, producing the results of what David Sereda calls *differentials* in his book *Differentials: The Hidden Harmonic Codes of the Universe*. Sereda explains that all things consist of vibrational frequencies which manifest as wavelengths of energy called waveforms. The interaction of differing wavelengths of opposing, counter-rotational waveforms, will always produce a manifestation which is "left over" from their differences as a result of their interaction. The interaction between the pair of opposites will always produce a resultant manifestation that did not exist prior to the interaction. This new manifestation occurs because as the two opposing forces interact, the differential produces a vacuum force (vortex), or torsion field that draws in energy from the zero-point void. The manifestations created by differentials are analogous to coherent superpositions of two reciprocal degrees, such as 70 percent *on* and 30 percent *off* on a dimmer light-switch, as an example. The result is a new manifestation which is neither fully *on* nor fully *off,* but exists as its own proper degree of intensity.

In accomplishing Reality Engineering, we allow for *existing* energy patterns to become *restructured* in accordance with our *desired* energy patterns. The mind can become aware of the relationship between various waveforms and thereby observe them as interacting. But we are not seeking to produce differentials. We aim to completely replace the undesired reality with our intended reality. In this context, how can a specific reality be produced that is equivalent to the observer-participant's intention?

In Reality Engineering there are two opposing waveforms. The first is "the way things are," and the second is "the way the reality engineer intends them to be." By maintaining the intention charged with the completely heightened energy of its corresponding feeling, it creates a strong gravitational vacuum force, pulling the opposing reality of "the way things are" beyond the fringes of time, demoting it out of physical reality, and making it uninfluenced by the normal laws of physics. The empowered intention which was simultaneously maintained, instantaneously comes out of the vacuum and into existence, replacing the prior reality.

The engineer's belief in the new intended reality had been heightened to the degree that there doesn't exist a differential that will produce some hybrid of the two. The intention of the engineer *totally disbelieves in the "truth" of—and thereby the existence of—the opposing unwanted reality,* removing his attention and awareness of it. The new intended reality manifests itself triumphantly from the timeless realm of the Universal Mind because it proved to be more convincing than the original reality. Since two opposing realities cannot exist simultaneously in the same universe, and since nature abhors a vacuum, the waveform that is more "real" must replace the old or weaker reality.

In our observer-created universe, selecting an intention is equivalent to selecting from the infinite amount of waveforms, or infinite amounts of possible realities. The forces which allow interaction between our intended waveform and an existing waveform to shape reality are the *intensity of belief* and *emotion* which accompany the *intention* selected. So, until the original waveform is completely cancelled out through sufficient belief and emotion, our intended reality will not fully manifest in our consensus reality, and the differing waveforms will produce a differential that is left over from your manifestational efforts. The full and exact intention would only be a latent and unrealized possibility.

Once the intention ("the possibility") is selected, enough power of belief and feeling can then draw in its opposite to create the manifestation ("the new reality") equivalent to the intention. This is the black hole phenomenon. For example, when you mentally visualize something, *every element of your visualized blueprint is composed of a pattern of energy which will interact with the existing reality.* The idea is to create enough vibrational tension to *out-picture* the existing reality, and produce a new reality based on your new design. Though you may have selected the elements of your visualization, this alone is not strong enough to pull the sufficiently required quantum particles into your design, where they would re-combine and re-pattern themselves according to your visualization.

This is accomplished by directing one's intention. But, as you are directing intention, your belief must reach the level of complete certainty, plus the emotion and feeling which fully supports the conviction of the new reality. Sereda explains that the opposing strain of these interacting waveforms cause a *pull* to open up a rift of negative-magnetism between them, or at the center of their interaction. This is the doorway allowing consciousness to access the vacuum of the Universal Mind where reality can be modified by the intention. Now let me show you how to do this.

Auto-Suggestion

Suggestion is the process by which a physical or mental state is influenced by a thought, idea, or expression thereof. No one can deny that this occurs to them every day in one way or another. *Auto*-suggestion, on the other hand, is of particular interest to us because it makes it possible for us to influence our own selves in ways that do not depend on anything exterior to ourselves. Our power of choice becomes the sole determining factor. Auto-suggestion is the process by which we make ourselves believe whatever we choose to believe.

There are two things to remember in order to employ auto-suggestion properly. First, it is ineffective to keep suggesting to yourself that you *will* have something, especially when that suggestion is accompanied by the feeling of not yet having it. In such a case, that time will never come. That thought suggests a future event. If you continue having the thought of a "future having," *the having will remain in the future.* The present will keep coming up short of reaching it. To achieve your intended results with regard to events or situations that have a particular future day and time, one's expectation has to reach the level of believing that it is *now* a done deal, and you must see and feel yourself in that future event *as if it were happening now.* In order to get and have particular results now, you must use *present-tense* and have them *Now!*

Second, the use of the *positive-tense* is also required. Don't tell Infinite Intelligence what you *don't* want or have. Don't say *"I'm not a miserable person," "I don't want to be poor anymore," "I'm not sick,"* etc. These are statements of negation which give visuals of the undesired state, thereby reinforcing it. Tell a child *"Don't go into the street,"* and that child will go into the street when you're not looking. Instead give the child a visual of the sidewalk, *"Stay on the sidewalk."* Express only the positive aspect of having. Say *"I am happy, prosperous, and healthy."*

Many who have tried using auto-suggestion and have encountered difficulty in getting results did so due to the following reasons:

- They wavered in their power of belief;

- The belief was not accompanied by the emotion and feeling necessary to carry it to the super-conscious mind; or

- They failed to use the present/positive tense.

Any of these factors may have been due to a lack of understanding of their learned technique.

The concept of auto-suggestion teaches us that nothing outside of ourselves was ever meant to be the primary influence of our lives. We've always had this ability and always will. Regardless of what may befall an individual, if you have the power to think, all things are possible for you. Even complete paralysis of the body is not a bar. A person may be shut from the world as far as communication goes, but if such a person is still aware of his or her thoughts—that's all he or she needs as a starting point to improve their life condition. There have been numerous terminal cases that, with the power of the mind, were able to beat all of the odds that appeared to be stacked against them.

What roles do belief and emotion have in all of this? Altering our perception or beliefs transmits distinct signals to our cells, leading to a reprogramming of their expression. It is for this reason that individuals are experiencing spontaneous remissions or recovering from injuries previously considered permanent disabilities. A fascinating experiment conducted by Dr. Glen Rein shows that when we induce emotions within us, particularly the emotions of unconditional love and appreciation, these emotions significantly influence our DNA, transforming the molecule in a positive manner. This discovery is quite significant considering the fact that our bodies consist of trillions of such molecules which make up our very genetic blueprint. When the emotion of love was present in Dr. Rein's experiment, the DNA was seen to unwind and expand. This unwinding allows the DNA molecule to open up and thereby change or rearrange its informational content.

Biologist Barbara McClintock discovered that these changes were occurring within the larger part of the DNA molecule which previously had been considered to have no function. She found that about a million distinct proteins—named *transposons*—within the DNA have the ability to shift over to other locations in the DNA, thereby restructuring it. Undoubtedly, the movement of these DNA proteins are what make miraculous healings occur. Our ability to affect our DNA with our intentions, in the form of beliefs and emotions, prompt these proteins to readjust our genetic blueprint. Negative intentions picked up by our DNA will bring about illness, disease, and deformities, whereas positive intentions will do the opposite.

These transposons appear as if they have an intrinsic intuition all on their own, when in fact Infinite Intelligence is the guiding force behind them. The omnipotence of the mind has the intelligence to know where and how to rearrange our genetic code according to whatever signal we send down the Reciprocal Circuit via subtle energy force. Once the power of auto-suggestion acts upon our DNA, *all* of the DNA molecules within our bodies transform simultaneously. Depending on your intent, whether the transformation occurs over a month or instantaneously, the *Holographic Principle* (which states that a *part* will contain and directly correspond with the qualities and properties of the *whole* to which it belongs) will be operative in allowing all of the DNA molecules to change in unison. Incidentally, the same changes occurring to your DNA within your body will occur simultaneously to a DNA sample of yours that is contained in a tube being observed by scientists miles away. The non-local nature of the mind makes this possible, the mind having authority over space and time. This is also why healing at a distance can occur with such rapidity.

You may already have been aware of the fact that a mind-body connection exists, and that auto-suggestion can influence the body in both positive and negative ways, which may account for the unexplained illnesses and miraculous recoveries we sometimes hear of. But, what does this have to do with influencing the outcome of external reality? Let us consider the world beyond our bodies in light of what we have already covered.

If our beliefs and emotional states can influence our DNA, and our DNA in turn can influence light particles that exist independently outside of the body (as in the *DNA Phantom Effect*), then it logically and logistically follows that our emotions can influence the "external" building blocks of matter through the unimpeded medium of subtle energy. Since all matter is composed of energy ($E=mc2$) consisting of wave-like patterns that are susceptible to our subjective interaction and influence, we can therefore influence anything in the material universe, *limited only by the direction of our own subjective processes.*

Method Acting

A magician is an actor playing the part of a magician.

The performer must sufficiently enter into the part he plays, to himself believe in the reality of his fictitious statements.

This belief on his own part will infallibly carry a like conviction to the minds of the spectators.
—Robert-Houdin (1805-1871) Magician

In the acting profession the most extreme, though highly respected, form of acting is called *Method Acting*. By using this technique, an actor seeks to reach total identification with the inner personality of the character that is being portrayed. The actor essentially *becomes* the character by *believing* himself or herself to actually *be* the character. It would be quite unreasonable to refer to these people as delusional or somehow mentally deranged. We understand the fact that it is part of their job to portray characters as convincingly as possible.

I bring this topic to your attention in order to illustrate the concept used in the method described in this book. Yet, the technique I present goes further than method acting, because it does not limit itself to the process of *being*, but includes *doing* and *having* in any area of life that isn't limited to a Hollywood script.

An acquaintance of mine sent me the following account illustrating the wrongful use of the Reciprocal Circuit:

"Many years ago I had a friend named Carlos who worked with me. He secretly confided with me and a couple of our other friends that he planned to fake wrist and forearm pain in one of his arms in order to eventually collect compensation from our employer. He went through the entire act of going to his doctor, feigning nerve pain, and obtaining a wrist and forearm brace allowing him to work. Day after day, week after week, month after month, he allowed himself to be seen wearing the brace,

71

and every once in a while would put on his pain act whenever he would remove the brace.

"One day the four of us decided to get together and go have a nice friendly dinner out. As Carlos arrived at the table, he takes off his jacket and I notice that he is wearing his brace. I sort of laugh and tell him that there's no need for him to wear that around us, *"or did you just forget to take it off?"* I asked. He turned to look at me with a puzzled, yet serious look on his face and said *"What do you mean? I do need to wear it."* After reminding him of his plan to collect by faking the injury, he says *"No. It's true. My wrist and forearm are really messed-up, and funny thing, I don't know how it happened!"* Taking off the brace, he showed us a very feeble left arm in comparison to his right arm, and then demonstrated excruciating pain as he tried to pick up his chair with his left hand."

Carlos had used the circuit to his disadvantage without even realizing it. He received exactly what he sent down the circuit. He convinced his conscious mind to the degree that the super-conscious mind accepted it as a reality, and it thereby produced it for him and everyone else to see. Were they all delusional?

In no way would I ever suggest that you do anything like what Carlos did. Let it serve as an example of what *not* to do, while at the same time showing you how powerful the mind really is.

Revisiting Your Central Belief System

There are significant beliefs about life that you hold which tend to define who you are. These are the most difficult to change. Yet, you may find that they've been indirectly called into question as you practice the exercises in this book. You must be willing to challenge not only the validity of these beliefs if they limit you somehow, but also their very usefulness.

For instance, what view do you have about the opposite sex? What led you to have that perception? Is it preventing you from fully being who you want to be? Whatever your answer may be, realize that whatever you hold as true will be so in your life. So, holding the view that *"all men are insensitive"* will attract to you men that are somehow or another insensitive. Always keep in mind that no matter how deep-set your notions are about life and the things in it, you can change them. If you continue believing that you are an unlucky person, or that you have a family curse, or that other people always mean you harm, then these are what you will continue to bring into your life. What are your beliefs about money, the future, and your health?

You must continuously modify your central belief system and seriously consider modifying it until the useless and damaging beliefs are eradicated. Stop clinging to them as if they are protecting you somehow. They are not. They are actually perpetuating the very things that they proclaim, and preventing you from realizing your full potential.

Quick Method

Take a limiting belief and extend it in front of you (or step back from it) and observe it independently until you realize the truth of the matter, being freed from that particular belief's power over you.

Luis Mantoris

Believe it Now!

What is truth?
—Pontius Pilate, Roman Procurator of Judea (1st century AD)

Nothing is true. Everything is permitted.
—Hassan I Sabbah (b. 1034—d. 1124)

Belief And Momentum

*You must get up to speed with the vibrational frequency
of a belief before you can tap into its power.*

In order for the adoption of a new belief to become manifest, that new belief must rise to the level of a certainty. Knowing for certain that something is true is a vital ingredient to manifestation, whereas doubt will nullify it.

Three very important basic beliefs to adopt are:

- I have instant access to absolutely anything and everything at all times;

- My desired reality is already a fact; and

- I'm creating it all.

When you emit a signal to the super-conscious mind, the factors that comprise the signal must be accompanied by the belief that you in fact already have that which you desire. The very fact that we possess a spiritual nature that is omnipotent guarantees that everything is available to us. The "signal" consists of the mindset that it *won't fail because it cannot fail*—all we have to do is definitively *decide* that we already have it. Therefore, every time we say that we *need* something in our lives, not only are we affirming that we do not have it, but we are affirming it with an emotional concern that we may not get something that we must have. You cannot have anything by acknowledging your need of it. *Having* and *needing* are contradictory vibrations. You can only have something by *having it!* You might say "But, I *don't* have it, that's why I need it." Precisely. Those two statements will always go hand-in-hand. We create truth, it is a product of our omnipotent mind. You can make true any concept whatsoever.

In order to adopt a desired belief you must begin to act *As If you already have that particular belief.* Act *As If* you have absolutely no doubt in that belief. This act is not so much for others, but for you. The act will involve how you *behave* as well as what you *think* and *feel*.

With the material in this book you are developing a more empowering way of looking at reality. Your old way of thinking was not getting you the results you wanted. Change the method and you change the results. So, as you do the exercises, *know* that you have your desired result already, *have absolutely no doubt,* and genuinely accept it as a *fact*. Ignore any feeling of awkwardness. This will be a temporary feeling that will subside as you persist.

There are two basic ways of going about using your power of belief in connection with manifestation:

- Drafting your own specific blueprints of reality (which will be covered later); and

- Trusting in the Infinite Intelligence of Divine Providence.

The second method is very powerful on its own. It doesn't require visualization skills as the first method does. It does require a *knowing trust* so genuine and deep that your absolute belief in it is completely unshakable. The trust is put on the fact that Infinite Intelligence knows exactly what is needed at any given time and in any given situation, and that this divine power has unfailingly provided all that is needed despite any appearances to the contrary, as the first basic belief mentioned above states. In this state of belief, though the world around you may present to you undesirable situations, you trust that within the fabric of such appearances, everything is intelligently sewn for the provision of your utmost benefit, even if at that moment you don't see why or how it could be so. You genuinely trust that it is so.

Believing in What You Desire

If you initially do not believe in a desire that you have, don't let that discourage you from pursuing it, because the fact that you have the desire *at all* is unequivocal proof that the universe can deliver it to you, and that is all the evidence you need to begin pursuing the development of the belief in your desire.

To bring yourself to believe in your desire, you must continually think about your desire with *an undivided mind.* Though your desire and belief may be divided, at least you have a starting point of focus: *the desire.* First make your desire undivided while ignoring whatever your current contradictory belief in it may be. During this process, the universe will be working behind the scenes to remove the division between your desire and your belief in it. In other words, because you are now in a state of focus that you have chosen, your thoughts concerning your desire should not make you feel good in one moment, then bad in the next moment. Explore all the reasons that you want it, without touching upon why you *don't* or *can't* have it. Visualize what it would look like, and feel what it would feel like to have what you want. Make this process a joyful experience, and don't veer off track with the thought of *I'm trying to make something happen.* The thought of *trying* only confirms and supports the current reality of not having it. Such a thought keeps the desire and belief *divided*. Simply enjoy your desire as you continually consider it.

Just because you initially don't believe that you can or will have it, doesn't mean that you can't focus your thoughts about your desire in ways that feel good. When you do this consistently, the Universal Mind will attach to your original thoughts more thoughts related to your desire, blending with, and confirming them. This process helps you to form new and improved thought patterns that lead to a clearer view of what you desire, a clarity which allows for you to begin believing in it, and thereby increasing your enthusiasm for it. Eventually, as you continue to do this, evidence indicating the unfolding of your desire begins to show up, adding even more support to your growing belief that your desire is not only possible, but probable.

Allow the momentum to continue to build until you strongly believe in the fulfillment of your desire, and your belief is now up to par with your strong desire. Belief and desire are now vibrating at the same frequency, and are no longer separate and divided. At this stage, your belief will have developed from a probability to a certainty. Under such conditions, the manifestation of your desire becomes inevitable because you have removed all (or most) vibrational resistance to its realization. This occurs because your continual focus builds a battery of belief that becomes increasingly charged, until it gives life to your desire.

Performing this process may make you feel as if you are "in denial" of your current reality, but this is how beliefs are habitually and unknowingly formed anyway. Forming beliefs knowingly and with purpose will bring about a reality that you won't want to deny.

Feel it Now!

All of our moods are created by what we think about, the way we look at and perceive things, what we believe, the way we interpret things, and what we say about someone or something to ourselves. We can therefore *intentionally induce* specific emotions with our thoughts and beliefs. Just as we can select what to *believe* in by choice, we can do likewise with *emotions*.

The energy that issues forth from the heart is a very influential field of subtle energy that consists of an emotional quality. You can induce strong emotions within this field, and by doing so dramatically boost your ability to fully accept a chosen belief that has been associated or attached to that particular belief-supporting emotion. The heart's energy center is a spinning vortex of this subtle energy that has no limit to its periphery, expanding and embodying, at your will, anything that you associate with it. *The feeling convinces.* Without the power of this conviction, all of our wishes and dreams prove to be sterile.

It is important to know how to consciously feel. Feeling can be learned and utilized at will. This is done quite deliberately with purpose and direction. The transition that you are making is from being a person whose feelings get thrown and tossed by everyday happenings, to a person who can withstand the hurricanes of unforeseen occurrences, unthwarted and in total control of your emotional state. Your emotions and their associated physical sensations are tools of greater value to you than you may have ever thought.

Practical Body-Brushing

Brushing the body is a fundamental practice that will enhance your ability to feel. Get yourself a long-handled brush made of natural hair and that is suitable for brushing your body. You should brush your body on a daily basis, avoiding very sensitive areas such as your face. Do not brush too hard nor too soft. The best time to do this is when your skin is dry and before showering because in addition to making your skin more sensitive—which will increase your communication with, and awareness of your skin—you are also exfoliating dead skin cells which you should wash away. Brushing the skin in this manner also assists the body in eliminating impurities that exist within the body. The process takes about five minutes.

Your skin breathes, and body-brushing allows the pores of your skin to be more open and active. This activity allows you to be able to feel and sense your body more readily and easier than before. Having the ability to do this will speed your progress with the exercises in this book.

Emotional Engineering

Your emotions play a very significant role in the use of your omnipotent mind. Emotional engineering is the process of attaching a corresponding emotion to all other elements involved in designing the blueprint of your desired reality. Unwanted collateral results can be avoided by using the proper emotional ingredient to achieve results that you won't regret. The use of negative emotions and intentions will always produce undesirable results. This is the reason why I have placed the practice of examining your intentions at the forefront of this book.

Positive emotions are the only kind of emotions employed in emotional engineering. The basis for this is the fact that the very purpose for achieving anything in life is for it to contribute to the enjoyment of that life. Positive emotions are felt when we engage, or have the assurance of having, those things and circumstances that make us happy, content, joyful, and so on. Despite the appearance of loss of those things that contribute to that enjoyment, or the apparent threat of such loss, we in fact can never actually lose our ability to manufacture our own awareness of positive, uplifting emotions which will completely support the realization of any corresponding belief—and this emotion will be as real as we decide it to be.

Emotions are powerful sensations that are always accompanied by subtle energy force. At the time that the emotion is felt, this force then delivers all of the information that is embodied in the emotion to the super-conscious mind. If any emotion is present that indicates anything other than the fact that you are genuinely happy, then you will get results that will reflect that.

For instance if you desire to wed the person of your dreams while worrying that you don't measure up to his or her standards, then your emotion of *assured exhilaration* is commingled with *expectant inadequacy*, in which case you may very well end up marrying that person, but living a life under his or her thumb, belittling you and looking down upon you. On the other hand, if the emotion that accompanied your wish was that of *untainted exhilaration* and *unadulterated happiness*, then you would manifest a happy and fulfilling life with your new spouse.

The Reciprocal Circuit can be likened to the act of conception and procreation. The sexual urge *(intention)* of the male *(conscious mind)* implants a seed through the female's internal pathway of conception *(Reciprocal Circuit)*, carrying with it DNA *(information/reality blueprint)* into the fertile womb of the female *(super-conscious mind)*. The implantation takes place when extreme pleasurable sensations are experienced by the male *(conscious mind)*. The process occurring in the womb *(super-conscious mind)* is hidden from view, but the result is a new creation based on the DNA *(information/reality blueprint)*. We call childbirth a miracle because the creation of a new life is so wonderful to us. When the mind creates using the Reciprocal Circuit, the results appear miraculous as well.

Nothing but good, uplifting emotions are worth entertaining as you do your mental work. The following exercise will help you immensely in securing the proper emotion:

Exercise Four

1. Begin by finding a quiet place where you won't be disturbed for the duration of your practice session.

2. Decide on a seated or lying position, whichever is most comfortable or convenient for you.

3. Close your eyes and become aware of your present emotion. Look at the emotion as if you were separate from it, as if you've stepped back and are now at a distance from it. You can do this because every emotion has a physical sensation associated with it along with its own breathing pattern. Watch the breathing pattern and the physical sensation that belongs to the emotion. You will know that you are doing this correctly if the emotion and breathing begin to change.

    (The I is what is looking at the emotion. By watching the emotion in observer mode, then you become totally uninfluenced by the emotion. The I can always choose to be influenced, uninfluenced (neutral), or the Influencer. This step is asking you to be neutral and uninfluenced by whatever the body is experiencing emotionally. The fourth step will ask you to be the Influencer.)

4. Consciously and deliberately create a rising sense of joy until it is as powerful as you can get it. Feel and believe yourself happier and happier. You can begin feeling the sensation of joy swelling up and outward from the area of

your heart center. At the same time, intentionally adjust your breathing to synchronize with your rising emotional quality of joy. Then hold your attention on the joyful emotion for as long as you can, feeling it all over your body as you continue to breathe. Become aware of as much sensation as you can, intensifying it. *(If you lose your grip on it, repeat steps three and four. Continue to repeat until you can easily enter this state of exhilaration and maintain it for at least fifteen minutes. This may take more than one session so don't become easily discouraged. If you keep at it, success will be sure to come.)*

- In addition to happiness, you can add other positive feelings that contribute to happiness, such as *unconditional love, appreciation,* and *enthusiasm.* These are all very powerful and accomplish the aim of this exercise.

- *(For those that find it difficult to induce such a joyful emotion, try bringing to mind an experience that filled your heart with utter joy. Relive how you felt. Hold on to the feeling as you bring yourself to the present moment along with the emotion. This refamiliarizes you with the emotion which will be easier for you to feel with more practice.)*

5. This fifth step does not require a quiet place or a chair or bed. You are now to practice maintaining your uplifted state as you go about your everyday affairs, from when you wake up in the morning until you go to sleep at night. As you walk down the street, as you do your laundry, cook, work, bathe—everything. There may be times that you may forget or get distracted. If you do, just jump right back into it without the least bit of frustration or self-criticism. If an hour has passed by and you realize that

during that time you weren't "sticking to it," just *begin anew* with no sense of failure whatsoever. That time will shorten with practice.

Achieving stability with this state of emotion doesn't just make you a happier person, it also gives you the invaluable ability to achieve this state at will. You will become undisturbed when confronted by events that would have rattled you in the past. You are more in control of your actions and your thoughts. You can make wiser decisions that aren't based on the limiting emotions of fear, anger, hatred, or sorrow. Your life in general will be more enjoyable. Things that do not conform to your newly-found happiness will begin to leave. Some of these things may appear to get worse just before they leave—but *they will leave* as long as you maintain a genuine undisturbed attitude of true happiness. *Know* that you are happy and it will be so. If at any time your thoughts try to convince you that there are reasons why you should not be happy, dismiss the thought immediately, do not let it take root. Just take back the control of your emotional state.

Continue doing this until it becomes difficult for you to feel angry or sad, whereas it may have been quite easy in the past. It should be natural for you to be happy. You will have achieved this by simply *intending* to do so. Eventually you will be able to extend the vibration of happiness to your environment by intending it as well. Elements that are not in sync with this vibration will be repelled by it and they will seek out other vibrational patterns that will accept them, and the overall conditions in your life will improve.

Appreciation and Relief

The feeling that most strongly convinces us of "having it now" is genuine appreciation and relief. When you are elevating your emotional level, combine it with the strongest sense of appreciation and relief that you can generate. Making these two qualities a part of the signal you send through the Reciprocal Circuit will strongly galvanize your belief of your actual possession of your desire. When you feel true appreciation for something that you previously wanted, the reason usually is because you are relieved that you have now received it. So, feel a great sense of sincere appreciation and relief knowing it's already yours, and you will believe that you in fact have it.

Appreciate and feel relieved that everything is always available to you and that this particular object or circumstance is what you are acknowledging as having now. Know and believe this at all times until it is a firm part of your belief system. Your expected outcomes will then arrive easily enough. To simplify this, just ask yourself "How appreciative and relieved would I feel if I in fact had this at this moment?" When you *feel the answer* to that question, heighten it and use that very same feeling when you do your exercises. This doesn't just apply to material possessions, but also to life situations that you desire to have.

Joyously assert your appreciation for anything that you desire, knowing you already have it despite all appearances to the contrary. Totally ignore these appearances. Know that it is true and sincerely express it verbally, feeling it with every fiber of your being: *I am so happy that I have* _____! *I am so thankful for* _____! Look at yourself in the mirror, and with all the enthusiasm you can muster, proclaim that you in fact do have it. These aren't just dry affirmations that you repeat over and over again hoping that they sink deep into your subconscious. They must be living statements that are full of energy and conviction, enlivening the concepts embedded within them.

There is a practice of spoon-bending which utilizes the act of yelling out the word *bend* as the person holds a spoon in-between the palms of both hands lengthwise. Subtle energy, in the form of a ball of white light, is made to travel back and forth from one hand, through the spoon, to the other hand. The speed of the traveling energy is made to reach a rapid pace at which time the person begins to yell loudly at the spoon *Bend!!! Bend!!!*

This is not a criticism against spoon-bending, because, depending on how well the individual performs the technique, the spoon will actually bend, and sometimes become quite easily deformed. The "trick" is that as one yells, there is *a strong surge of emotion released* from the person. The heightened emotion, plus the consciously activated subtle energy, and the intention of "bend" directed at the spoon were enough ingredients to alter reality. The *Kia* yell used in the martial arts in order to direct power punches while using *chi*, or internal (subtle) energy, as well as yells used in intense sports activities, are also examples of using this yelling method.

I don't suggest you go around yelling in this manner because the release of the strong surge of emotional energy can be accomplished without doing so. Besides, the above technique of spoon-bending is usually used as a quick demonstration for new practitioners of particular modalities to try so that they can experience the power the mind has over matter.

Personal Magnetism

Not only are you repelling unwanted things in your life, but you are also drawing to you things that contribute to your happiness. You have become a living magnet. As you increase this positive emotion, you increase the conscious reach of the subtle energy force that accompanies it. This force has a vibrational quality which, by means of the magnetic law of mind, will bring to you things of corresponding vibration. Heighten the emotional quality and your personal magnetism will strengthen as well, and in the background we have the super-conscious mind making it all possible.

On the flip side of the metaphorical coin, when a person has an emotional outburst, he or she is activating the very same mechanism described in the exercise, except for the fact that the person has become a magnet for hatred and anger. You may have noticed that many good, loving people will tend to be repelled by such a person, whereas people of the same hateful vibration will seek the negative person out for purposes of revenge or some other trouble. The more these outbursts occur, the more the person's life is full of negative things they don't want.

In order to maintain one's happiness, one must *continually induce* such happiness within oneself. Amidst a world of rampant conflict and betrayal it is does not make sense to rely on external things to be the source of true lasting happiness. We must take an active stance and recognize the true Source of consistent joy, our divine qualities and abilities. You can make *yourself* happy, thereby causing favorable conditions to be prevalent in your life.

The Beatitudes, or Happinesses, which appear in the New Testament (also found in Buddhist literature) teach this very concept. For instance: *Happy are those that hunger, because they will be filled.* At first glance this made very little sense to me. I rarely felt happy when undergoing hunger. The passage is really teaching that by joyfully knowing that your food is guaranteed despite your hunger, you are thereby attracting the food or circumstance that will eventually get your belly filled. Were you to be miserably and hopelessly hungry, you will simply attract more misery and more hunger.

See it Now!
Drafting Mental Blueprints of Reality

In chapter one you were asked to make up a list of things that you desire in order to avoid wasting any time trying to think of what you really desire in your life when you reach this part of the book. Your desires must be very clear in your mind. It is often suggested that you start with something simple and neutral in order to avoid feeling like a great failure if you don't seem to get it right at first and to avoid *lust of the result* interfering with the process.

Now, pick either a common item that you do not feel a great need for, or pick one of the items on your list. Whatever you choose, stick with it. This shall be the item you will work on as you go through the rest of this book, and until it shows up in your life. Then you may choose another item from your list. It is important that you actually witness your creations surface into reality. You will never be the same again when this happens to you. You step over a line, then when you turn to look, the line is gone—and everything else looks different.

The Power of Imagination

If you always considered your imagination as unreal, from this point forward dispel yourself of such a notion. The imagination is as real as anything else. To doubt its reality is to stifle its true potential. You can use your imagination not only to visualize, but also to hear, touch, taste, and smell. As was mentioned earlier, what you create in your imagination is accepted and treated as real by the super-conscious mind as long as *you* do not doubt it as a reality.

Exercise Five

1. Sit or lie down in a quiet place.

2. Close your eyes and begin to feel the positive emotions such as joy, love, appreciation, relief, and exhilaration, increasing the sensation in your body by increasing your breathing. Maintain this throughout the entirety of the exercise.

3. *Build a Mental Picture*—Mentally see clearly and vividly the object, person, or situation as if it is present with you right now! See only the end result, not how it might come to you. Give it its precise form and detail. You can hear it and touch it, even smell or taste it if these senses are involved. If it is a person, then have the consciousness that this person is aware of your presence as well. See it as a present fact. Feel your proximity to the contents of the image. Interact with it. Feel how you would feel if your image were a reality. Most of all, feel the appreciation that comes with receiving it. Eliminate any concept of separation between you and your imagery. You share the same space with it and exist in the same realm.

4. After thoroughly doing the above, you can open your eyes to a brand new world and say to yourself *I have it!* and continue going about your day with this conviction, not *Okay, so where is it?* nor *I will have it, if this thing works.* Know that you have it and continue knowing that you have it. It is a done deal regardless of so-called outward indications to the contrary. As soon as it makes its appearance you can then say *See, I told you I have it.* Know it to be true! Knowing it's yours, say the things that you would say in the actual presence of whatever your image is.

When visualizing, if the vision fades in and out, this is fine as long as you persist in recalling the image in order to make it clearer and clearer. Continue until you are satisfied with having seen it *now*. This is key because if you have any doubt that it is really in your presence now, then your super-conscious mind will pick up this doubt as a component of the signal you are sending to it. In that case, what you are basically telling super-consciousness is: *This image is not really here.* Then, when you look for the image as a reality in your life, you will only find that you *got* what you gave: *The image is not here.*

Also when visualizing, make sure to see in full color if you are able to do so, and also hear clearly any related sounds. Make the image as tangible as anything else you've ever touched. All of this will greatly contribute to your success at *viewing it as if it were truly present.* When you do, you establish an unimpeded connection with your omnipotent mind who only knows that what you desire is present, and it will validate this agreement by showing it to you in your reality. This is the cosmic mirror in full operation, reflecting back the exact image that you gave it. This is the mental law *as above, so below* being obeyed.

Using Photographs

A great aid in accomplishing the aim of visualization is the persistent and focused use of photographs. Get a photograph of *the end result* of what you desire. Place it somewhere that you will see it constantly every day. Before your actual practice, look at it intensely, capturing every detail necessary for your mental creation. Make the photographic image a three-dimensional reality in your mental imagery. Step into the picture, and make it real.

I heard a woman recount an experience that she had when she came across a book about the praying mantis. It turns out that she did not know what a praying mantis was, and she had never seen one before in her life. As she was riding on a bus looking at the cover photo of a praying mantis with its beautiful color shining off of it as the sun hit it, she was mesmerized by its appearance and her sight was glued to this image for a very long time on her trip back home. For a moment she felt as if she had lost her sense of time. When she got home, she entered the house, went to her upstairs bedroom, and found on her ceiling the very same beautiful praying mantis. This she found in a house that, as she recounted, has very well-screened windows, and she saw no way it could have entered her house. This mystery is compounded by the fact that she did not live in an area that was known to have praying mantis.

She may not know the process that she was involved in, but it is quite clear that this is no mere coincidence. Something happened as she lost herself in the focusing of the image, and in her heartfelt appreciation of it. Without knowing what a praying mantis looked like, she would not have been able to send an image of it down the reciprocal circuit and have it appear by means of the super-conscious mind.

Whenever possible, use full-color photographs to aid your imagination. Make sure it looks exactly like what you need or want. If you are unsure as to what its full details are, search for such a photographic image until you do find it. It will be worth your time and effort. Peruse related magazines and books, search the web, or go out and take your own photos!

Improve Your Visualization Skills

The following exercise is very useful for those who have very stagnant imaginative faculties, and for those who simply want to improve their current ability. An inactive imagination hinders creativity to a large degree. Practice using your imagination until it is easy for you to control your self-created images. The results you get from constant practice will prove to be invaluable. As the architect of your reality, you will be able to engineer and design your ideal life.

When you begin this exercise, you may not be able to hold on to an image for a few seconds. Keep repeating your efforts and you will notice that the more you train yourself this way, the longer the image will remain. Furthermore, at the outset, details of your image may be lacking. Continued efforts will also remedy this. Daily practice is vital, but don't rush it by skipping or doing incomplete steps. One of the goals is to visualize as vividly as possible, and as close to tangibility as you can. The exercise asks that you close your eyes. This would require that you record the exercise in order to play it back, or have someone read it to you. You can also try reading one step at a time, then closing your eyes to go through each step.

Exercise Six — Visualization Practice

1. Sit or lie down in a quiet place, and close your eyes and relax.

2. With eyes now closed, see *a pure whiteness* all around you in every possible direction and extending to the infinite depths of the universe. Practice this until you can hold it for at least five minutes.

3. When the white panorama has become easy for you to create, make a white medium-sized *ball* appear in front of you as if floating in mid-air. The ball should be in three-dimensional form.

4. Change the *color* of the ball to a violet color. Then practice changing it to any color you desire. When you find this

easy, pick a particular color and maintain that color on the ball for the rest of the exercise. If at any time you become bored with the color, change it, but do this consciously. If the ball changes its color without you choosing to do so, then you should make it a point to control this part of your visualization practice.

5. Now change the *size* of the ball by making it smaller, then larger, then smaller, then larger. When this has become easy, increase the speed gradually making it small then large then small, and so on. Then when the speed has become quite fast, lessen the speed gradually until the ball comes to a complete stop to its original size.

6. Make the ball move on its own, *up and down,* several feet slowly then speeding up. Continue increasing the speed as in the previous step until it is back where it started motionless. Repeat the same motion *side to side.* Make it go *around in a circle.* Lastly, make it move swiftly in *random directions* far and near, here and there at your discretion. When this is easy, return the ball to its original position in front of you.

7. Now make an *exact duplicate* of the ball right next to it. Allow them to play and move about in any manner you wish, making sure you maintain control of their movements without losing sight or track of them. When you feel comfortable with this ability, bring them back in front of you.

8. Make one of the balls *disappear.*

9. Adjust the *temperature* of the ball by making it as cold as ice. Feel the coldness as it emanates from the ball. Gradually warm up the ball until it becomes fiery hot, so hot it begins to glow. Bring it back to room temperature.

10. Reach out with your imaginary hands and tap the ball. *Feel and hear* what it would be like to do so.

11. As the ball floats in front of you, see it *split in half,* separating. It is now two halves of a hollow shell. Create a handful of beautiful multi-colored marbles and throw them in the shell. Close the two halves back together, sealing them with the marbles inside.

12. With your imaginary hands, take hold of the ball and *shake it.* Hear the marbles inside and feel them hit the inner surface of the ball.

13. Now *flatten* this ball perfectly until it takes the shape of a large smooth coin. Make the coin a shiny metallic piece hovering in front of you. Now *twist and stretch* this coin in any way you please. *Bend it, wiggle it, crunch it,* until this seems easy. *Reshape it* back to the original ball.

14. Now *hide* the ball behind you, then bring it back.

15. Imagine hundreds of arrows being shot at the ball from all directions, but you *shield it* with an invisible force-field that deflects them all.

16. Now make the ball completely *dissolve* into the white atmosphere. Then *reintegrate* all of the molecules back together again from where it went.

17. Reach out with your imaginary hands and hold the ball. Feel the light *weight* and change its weight gradually to a heavier weight, then back to a light weight. Feel the ball having a smooth *texture,* then a rough one, then a velvet feel to it, then sandpaper, then back to a smooth texture.

18. As you hold it, make it turn into a large *orange.* Feel the texture and temperature of this orange. Now smell it.

Split it in half and see all the detail that an orange should have. *Smell* the strong citrus, see the moist surface and the vibrant orange color. Hear the sound of the orange splitting in half clearly. Now bite into it and get its full *flavor* as you chew on it.

19. Close back the orange and make it turn back into a ball.

20. Make the ball change back to its original white color, then make it disappear completely.

The foregoing exercise should be practiced with various shapes (and fruit) at first. You should then use inanimate objects, such as household items. Then things you find in nature, such as plants, trees, rocks, water, etc. The purpose is to help you create and control your imagery. This exercise is more like a drill than an actual guided meditation. Feel free to devise similar exercises in addition to this one, but make sure to include the complete set of elements involved.

Putting it All Together

Resonating with the super-conscious mind in order to bring about specific outcomes in our reality requires the three components of *Belief, Imagination,* and *Emotion,* which together constitute the *Intention.* These must interact with each other in certain ways in order for your desire to manifest.

The awareness of the conscious mind focuses on an intention in which *belief, emotion*, and *imagination* play a part. These three always interact. That is why their adjustment and intensification are to be carried out in order to have your desire equate your definition of perceived reality. This intensification of *intention* is a stimulation of the subtle energy involved. The extent of the manifestation will depend on the fuel given to the subtle energy. The degree of stimulation will determine whether it will result in a mental, emotional, or a physical manifestation. Depending on the intention, combinations of all three may manifest. All three elements should be properly coordinated in order to accomplish the desired manifestation.

Creating a Virtual Reality Experience

The technique that I've outlined is most effective when you fully immerse yourself in your mental creation as if you were in a panoramic virtual-reality simulation. You would have an unobstructed and complete view of your image in every direction and from any angle you wish to view it. See everything as perfect as it should be. This exact duplicate only has the things you will have in your life, never the things you won't have.

Surround yourself with this clear and tangible three-dimensional creation, and surrender yourself to the existence of it. It is there and it is yours! Abandon all doubt and know that all of your mental creations are unequivocal evidence of what you already have. Commit yourself to this certainty and you will be able to bring about whatever you can mentally conceive. Allow your imagery to encompass you all around as if you were actually in the environment in which your desire will become a reality. If it is in the exact same spot in which you stand, then that is what you visualize, but experience it all in the *Now*. Think and know *This is happening to me right now!* Feel its presence. Hear the sounds, feel the textures, sense everything involved in your imagery. The closer to perfection it comes, the more super-consciousness accepts it as a reality to be given back to you in your life experience. The Circuit is there for all to use, and you are no exception, regardless of who you are.

The double-slit experiment which I mentioned in the first chapter was repeated again in 1998 by using more advanced technology. This more recent experiment not only confirmed the previous findings, but something else was noted. The more active the observer became in his observation, the more of a connection appeared to exist between the observer and the quantum particle. The observer's influence over the particle was magnified.

This is exactly what is happening when you become more involved in your mental creations—you are making stronger connections with the object of your intention, and the more you believe the connection is there, the more it is there. This is the difference between idly thinking about something, and fully immersing yourself in your mental imagery.

Chapter Six

Living the Solution

The super-conscious mind is always in operation, and it never rests or shuts down. Once you've seen results in your practice of the previous exercises, you may soon begin to realize that every single one of your thoughts and emotions are somehow reflected in your life experience. Wouldn't it be great if we can continue to use this power all the time and from here on out make our lives everything we would like it to be? Sure it would, and it can easily be done if you are willing to *live the solution to whatever may be "wrong" with your life.*

I must inform you that doing this will have the effect of changing who you are in a most positive way. This may seem similar to *Method Acting* which I described earlier in this book, with the difference that you will be improving your life the way you want it to be improved. You write your own life script and rewrite it as needed.

Living the solution is done in addition to the previous exercises. You will now begin to continuously maintain a *knowing* mindset, an attitude of *certainty* with regard to the thoughts that you have about everything in your life. You do this by choosing how your life is to be and you simply *decide* that it is so. Always accompany the thought-current with the emotions and feelings that support that reality. This should be done with specific objectives as well as with general mindsets of *peace, beauty, prosperity, health, success,* and so on. Remember that there are no limits. The emotions of *love, happiness, exhilaration, ecstasy, relief,* and *appreciation,* should be called up at will in your everyday life, and should be dominating factors at all times. Sustaining these mental certainties and emotional states at all times, come what may, will act as a powerful magnet for the things you would like to have in life.

In addition to the above, you must begin to perceive and interpret your world differently. You cannot hold on to love and happiness very long if you are a habitually judgmental person. You must overcome this disposition by not allowing anything to bother you. Your main task from here on out is to see only *perfection* in your world, see only the things that *should* exist and nothing else. If you see anything wrong in your world, then that is what you will continue to invite and attract. The moment that you detect that you are criticizing or judging someone or something, transmute the thought and the feeling immediately to that which is worthy of your life experience. You're not just doing this to make yourself feel good, you are actually affecting sub-atomic particles the moment you change your mental and emotional direction. The super-conscious mind is making sure that these particles realign themselves perfectly according to your signal of intent. You can be assured that *whatever occurs* as you maintain the requisite state of consciousness, is the resulting manifestation of your omnipotent mind's Supreme Intelligence. As you witness this Intelligence choreograph events in your life, acknowledge it with sincere relieved appreciation. Everything that you can ever experience can only appear on the strength of this Intelligence. As you tune into it, you become a conscious participant. Never question what you see, just recognize its source knowing that what you are experiencing is what you need to experience.

Commitment and persistence are vital in living the solution because it is a way of being that goes against the flow of our society, which, in general, is *living the problem.* They see so much wrong with the world, with their marriages, their jobs, their health, the environment, the government, and the future. It is their very negative thoughts, emotions, and beliefs that hold these problems in place. They expect to see and experience all these defects and that is exactly what they get. They will continue to receive what they put forth.

Exercise Seven

1. Decide right this instant that you will not allow anything to ever disturb your peace of mind, seeing beauty all around you, knowing that you always have everything you need—never notice that you don't have whatever it is. Feel and know that you have it. Know that your world is a world of peace despite any appearance to the contrary. Be continuously relieved and appreciative of all of this.

2. If at any time your disposition or attitude gets out of focus due to a distraction, as soon as you realize what has happened, just jump right back into the same stream of thought without evaluating or thinking of the reasons why the object of distraction is "more important." Ignore the fact that you were distracted. You will see that whatever it was can be handled more effectively with your higher state of mind.

   [* *There may be a persistent negative feeling in the body due to emotion or physical pain. Allow the true you, the I, to sort of step back and observe this feeling without being engaged in it nor allowing it to bother you in any way. The very act of observing it in a detached manner will begin to have a transformative effect on it and your relationship to it, just as in the scientific experiments. It is "thought" that has been holding it in place—it is "thought" that can remove it.*]

The *I* can decide to be in whatever state it wants to be in, as long as it doesn't get lost and entangled in the limiting emotions and discomforts of everyday life. It can step back and observe the entire body all at once (it can also do this extending outside of the body to the far reaches of the universe). When this is done, you'll feel the body as a whole unit undergoing different sensations. You are experiencing the body's natural intelligent process of healing itself and functioning the way it should without the mind's usual interference to slow it down or misdirect it toward disease. You may actually feel a heightening of pain in certain areas of your body. Patiently allow for this as you entertain only good thoughts and feelings, totally undisturbed and unaffected by whatever else may be occurring. Normally the mind struggles to suppress this pain in order to accommodate its own comfort-zone. Stand firm as an observer with joyful appreciation. When this appreciation is genuine, there is no struggle to achieve it.

Your very observation makes your omnipotent mind not merely a participant, but the controlling factor. You can do this anytime you're confronted with situations that tend to force your thoughts or feelings to feel things that have no place in your ideal world.

3. When bedtime comes, go to sleep and wake up the next day determined to maintain your new character.

4. Throughout your day, as you encounter needs and wants, adopt these into the mindset of *already have it,* and have absolutely no doubt about this. Remember the powerful changes you are effecting in the quantum field the moment you do this.

Make this a habit day after day and it will become second nature to you, and you will have reestablished your connection with your omnipotent mind.

The key to *living the solution* is to never foster any negative or limiting thoughts or emotions. You are a being that already has everything—therefore act like it, think like it, and feel like it at all times. Let this permeate every fiber of your existence. Disregard anything that tends to indicate otherwise. Don't be judgmental of such things, just step back from it and it will have no adverse effect on you. When you have aligned your beliefs and emotions, and are actually seeing with your physical eyes (not just your imagination) your ideal world, you will be resonating with super-consciousness. When this resonance is based on a full *living of the solution,* the super-conscious mind will solve all of your problems, and it will bring to you everything that coincides with your ideal. When it sees that you are thinking and feeling as an omnipotent being, it will then provide what is necessary to prove that you are that being!

Love thy Enemy?

> *I saw an angel in the marble and carved until I set him free.*
> —Michelangelo

You may ask how it may be possible to not have hatred or resentment for someone that deliberately wrongs you or is a heartless enemy. This concern is not an unreasonable one, but not one without solution.

One of the basic attributes of the immortal spirit is a strong sense of order. Antipathetic individuals in your life will do things to aggravate that intrinsic quality. Limited thinking in this matter will only produce limited solutions. Therefore, view this from the perspective of your omnipotent mind by doing the following:

1. First, stop mentally mulling over whatever has been done to you. Unless you do, it will be nearly impossible for you to see beyond your anger.

2. Then remind yourself that:

- Those people exist in your life because you somehow attracted them;

- Their negative attributes are flimsy illusions, or rather, false conditions which you are continually creating with your own negativity; and

- Replacing your own negative condition with a positive one will repel such people and attract true friends (or attract the hidden friend that exists *within* that "enemy"). This is done by seeing, or creating, the desired conditions. When you acknowledge and take responsibility for the part you are playing as the creator of your current experience, only then will it be easy for you to see the desired condition which is found just beyond the undesired existing condition.

Constantly dwelling on what the other person *should have done* or *should not have done*, will keep you stuck in a seemingly unsolvable cycle of anger, animosity, revenge, and regret. You remain in victim-mode. Religious dogma aside, it is true that by loving someone unconditionally, you allow no room for hatred. Yet, you may find it easier to first adopt a *neutral* stance in order to control your emotions to the point of having *no-hatred* and *no-anger.* Each time that you accomplish this, you approach your omnipotent mind more and more because you are thereby letting go of your victim mindset. An all-powerful being can never be a victim.

You can eliminate hatred without actually "loving" harmful things, people, and events. In fact, when you love someone who has wronged you, you are not loving the enemy that wrongs you, but you are allowing yourself to see beyond such behavior to the person beneath the illusion of "enemy," which is *the perfect individual you have been choosing not to see.*

Eliminating hatred of your enemies is such a powerful process that you need never tell them that you adopted such a disposition towards them. In *not-hating* them you are avoiding attracting into your life further experiences of hatred. By sending the signal of hatred through the Reciprocal Circuit, you would be asking that hatred be returned to you somehow.

When you have gotten the knack of *not-hating,* the next step you should take is *forgiving.* Forgiving is remarkably easy and will prove to be the most rewarding thing you will have done for yourself. The release you end up feeling will open your eyes to life like you've never seen it before. Genuine forgiveness should be done within yourself and without the *need* for the other person to apologize to you. This process will have an effect on the other individual due to the non-local nature of the mind, but it is that other person's responsibility to deal with that aspect of his or her life. You've done your part.

In addition, *eliminate resentment and guilt from your life.* Resentment and guilt are very poisonous conditions preventing you from living your life to the fullest. They have an adverse effect on the physical body, as well as being social traps that you will do well to release yourself from. Forgiveness is the cure for resentment and guilt. Unless you truly forgive, guilt will continue to grip you fiercely. To continue this way is to allow your emotions to control you. On the other hand, when you allow unconditional love to play the key role in your life, you stand before the door of true divine power. Break these bonds *for yourself* and you will see how easy it is to break them *with others,* and vice versa. You must start somewhere.

Loving without conditions allows for genuine forgiveness to be possible. Our divine inheritance comes with the ability to love without the need to have something returned to us. Doing so does not mean that the individual automatically becomes trustworthy. It means that you love the individual *despite* his or her apparent imperfections because you are no longer *seeing* those imperfections. Keep in mind that the perfected individual does indeed exist beneath the outer experience in which he or she is operating. We pull that person to our outer experience by our transformed perspective. Our perspective is a subjective, yet powerful one. We forgive with a purpose, understanding that the process is based on an unfailing law.

If you find it very difficult to reverse the ill-will you have against someone, if you are too angry or hurt to forgive, do not give up. In order to help you overcome such a seemingly impenetrable barrier, I suggest that you employ the following technique: *Act As If!* Just like *method acting* mentioned in chapter five, *acting as if* allows you to experience how easy it is to change your feelings about somebody. Once you try it you will realize that you can reclaim the power that you unknowingly gave to the other individual. If it is a person that you must cross paths with on a regular basis, then they will also notice that their power over you has vanished. This may expose the true individual or it may have the effect of repelling that person until he or she is no longer a factor in your life, or until one day you notice that they are just "not there anymore".

This involves pretending to the point that you behave, talk, and feel as if such a person has absolutely no disturbing effect upon you. Do this in their presence and in their absence, maintaining this disposition until you feel comfortable feeling what you are feeling, then you are no longer pretending.

Unconditional love is just one part of *living the solution*. I would rather say *The more love you have, the more friends you will attract*. In reality, you make your own enemies. It is also true that you can conceive just about anything as your enemy, including yourself. These are mental creations that can easily be undone by simply choosing to do so. That's why *living the solution* is so effective: anything that contains an enemy-factor is a problem that can be systematically solved using the *law of mind.*

Seeing Perfection

Father of talismans, keeper of wonders.
[*The Tablet*—Passage 5]

The word in the text of the *Emerald Tablet* which has been translated as *talismans,* is a word referring to *consecrations.* To consecrate is to *completely and perfectly endow something with the qualities and properties for the purpose with which it is intended.*

Not only is this how talismans are made, but it is also why everything around you exists. The mind is the father of all of these "talismans" that you see around you. The mind consecrates all of life's talismans with their own particular meanings and purposes for which they exist. To be fully convinced of the attributes of something is to have made your talisman *complete.*

Examples of talismans are amulets, money, and even one's spouse. Unfortunately, many of the things in our lives have been endowed with, or given properties and qualities that are not in accord with our inherent divine perfection, but have been given complete attributes of negativity and imperfection. Since it is the subjective mind that does this, it is the subjective mind that can also see perfection in all things.

The concept of seeing perfection in everything may sound like an impossible task to you, but keep in mind that an omnipotent mind must only see perfection as the absolute truth underlying everything in existence because it cannot acknowledge the creation of a flawed product. Whenever the mind stops seeing perfection, its conscious power diminishes and enters a lower state of limitation which produces illusions of imperfection. Perfection is all around us, yet we cover up that perfection with a veil of imperfection. We disguise it with layers of concepts that deny the purity of creation. These concepts are what bring more imperfection into our lives. The beauty of life is thereby continually tainted with falsity.

We have the ability to see perfection all around us by denying the existence of imperfection. By doing so, you invite everything that a perfect world entails into your life. The reason this is possible is because the imperfection we see in the world is a self-created illusory view that simultaneously exists along with the truth of its perfection which lies just beneath it and out of view. Choose to see the perfection and only the perfection, and stop holding on to the illusion you've been creating and giving power to. In addition, contemplate the following: *How would it feel if I saw only perfection in everything?* Then immerse yourself in that attitude. Hold on to it as long as you can, then do it over and over again. You will notice that you are very capable of having tremendous amounts of unconditional love. This will feel very good to you because it is a feeling that is native to spirit, your true self. This love that you will feel as you see perfection all around you, will make *living the solution* a breeze.

Whenever you do this you are connecting with the Mind of the Divine. Adopting this view of your life experience places you in a position of great power, especially if you maintain it perpetually. You will attract ideal situations into your life. Whatever you consider to be optimal will find its way to you.

Real-Time Interaction with Thought-Forms

An advanced form of utilizing your imagination in order to attract what you desire is to do so interactively in real-time with thought-forms. This is like combining your imagination exercises with the process of *living the solution* as you go about your daily routine. The adoption of this technique will take a little courage and creativity on your part. To those around you, you may appear to be "out of touch" with reality. So, it is advised that you not be so obvious about it unless you are around people who understand what it is that you are doing.

Instead of closing your eyes and imagining the entire scenario within your mind, this technique requires that you actually see, feel, hear, taste, and smell the thing right there in your environment as *realistic holograms,* and in your possession.

For example, if it's a motorcycle you desire, go to your garage and see it there. Go up to it and touch it with your physical hands, feeling it very distinctly. You feel the coldness of the metallic surface and its contours, including any rubber or leather parts. In addition, appreciate that it *is* yours, and relief that you finally have it—which is much different than appreciating that it *will be* yours. Smell the upholstery, see all the details that it should have. Move it around and feel its weight. Straddle it and start it up. Feel it vibrating underneath you and smell its exhaust fumes. Honk the horn and rev it a few times. Turn it off and dismount it. Admire it with deep appreciation, and leave the garage still feeling that way, knowing it is still in there.

You may feel like a professional mime in doing this, except that mimes only go through the motions, they don't believe that they are in possession of the thing, much less have any appreciation for it.

The example above demonstrates how to place thought-forms in your reality. These forms are to be considered just as real as material forms. It is our belief and appreciation of their existence that creates the required resonance between the conscious mind and the super-conscious mind, allowing the desired manifestation to stream forth into our physical reality. The fact that we can create it in thought-form is a guarantee of its reality!

This is one way that distant healing is conducted. If you are interested in healing others who are not in your immediate presence, the process would begin with your belief that the person is right there in front of you and already healed. If you place your hands on the individual, you can feel them in tangible form. Your healing intention will immediately interact with the person.

Once, when I was away on business, I called my wife on the phone to find out how her doctor's appointment went. She said that her doctor told her that her blood test revealed an abnormal increase in her white blood cell count, and that to find its cause and rule out leukemia and the need for them to go into her bone marrow, she would have to take another blood test that would be more thorough. That night after the phone call, I imagined her lying in front of me as my hands felt her body, energetically connecting with her. This allowed for my intention of her healthy body to be conveyed via subtle energy force. As this was occurring, I also visualized balanced white and red blood cells within her body, believing in their existence at that very moment. Her blood was to be retaken the next day, and the following week she would find out the results. My wife calls her doctor the next week to find out that the results came back totally normal! There were no signs of an imbalance in her blood, no sign of infection, leukemia, or anything that would cause an overproduction of white blood cells. The doctor had no explanation for the sudden change. One day my wife has a very high count of white blood cells, and the next day she doesn't.

On another occasion, I received word that a friend of mine named Frankie had injured his head quite badly when he fell and hit his head on a cement wall and then again as he went crashing down to the cement floor. He was in a coma and bleeding in his brain which caused a hard-to-reach blood-clot. The prognosis did not look good at all according to the doctors who were getting ready to go inside his head in order to try and remove the clot. After hearing this I immediately visualized him in my presence lying down. I went into his brain, and saw the blood-clot dissolve away, leaving his brain in perfect order. This I did with the idea and feeling that it was occurring at that very moment. In my visualization he then woke up in front of me in good spirits, and we both were thankful for this. The next day I was told that the previous night Frankie had not only come out of the coma, but when a second MRI was taken just before the scheduled operation, the clot was rapidly dissipating. There was no need to perform the operation.

All of these techniques revolve around *intention*. When healing a person in such a manner, your intention is to effect the *healing*, and thereby change the *lack* of someone's health, not necessarily to have the individual *appear* in your life. You intend the *healing* and appreciate that it is taking place. The difference with the motorcycle visualization is the fact that your intention is the *appearance* and the *having* of the motorcycle, thereby changing your *lack* of the motorcycle.

Using thought-forms in real-time is very effective and should be utilized whenever you are not around individuals who are willing to admit you to an insane asylum. In fact, this is the very process that I used that first time to produce my orange. I not only visualized it, I also felt its weight, its texture and its cool temperature.

Public speakers can overcome stage fright and deliver successful speeches by actually delivering their speeches in front of an imagined audience, believing the people in the audience to actually be there. They hear them respond to what the speaker says, hearing them clap, making eye contact with them, and so on.

There is no limit to how you may decide to interact with your thought-forms in real-time. The very best athletes do it all the time. We see them and think *"What skill! He's such a natural."* We say the same about musicians and artists. Yet these individuals have discovered how to access this power, and they have adapted it to what they love doing most. You can do the same and apply it to anything you need in your life.

Sleep

Sleep is a carriage to the super-conscious mind. This fact is of great advantage to us because a large chunk of our lives is spent in the state of sleep. Those eight hours or so a night is an ideal time to implant the super-conscious mind with our intentions. During sleep the conscious mind is suspended along with our limiting comfort-zone. This means that there is no need for us to make specific conscious efforts during sleep. With normal waking consciousness out of the picture, the super-conscious mind is free to operate at its capacity. But its work will always be in accord with *whatever was on your conscious mind as you drifted off into sleep*. This thought will be anchored into the super-conscious world. This can be something *specific* that you desire to be manifested, or it could be a *general* feeling of joy, leaving it up to the Infinite Intelligence of your omnipotent mind to provide the details. Feel and believe yourself to be happy and having a happy, fulfilling life as you slip into your sleep. Whatever can bring you joy will appear in your other waking hours.

In the realm of the super-consciousness, linear time doesn't exist as we are accustomed to measuring it. All events past, present, and future exist in one accessible immeasurable moment. This is why our present-tense intentions can become reality when we place them in that realm. When we ignore the notion that something *needs time* to manifest, we are resonating with the mind's omnipotence, thereby activating its power.

It should go without saying that, regardless of the events of the day, never go to sleep in a bad mood or with a self-defeating belief. These will only make its impression upon the sub-conscious mind which will act upon every suboptimal thought and feeling that you present it with. More negativity will show up in your life, and nobody but yourself will be responsible for the manifestation.

Make sure that as you fall asleep, your dominant attitude is in accordance with what you desire in life. This attitude must be felt as a present reality—not as a reality you *want* to have, but as a reality you *now* have.

Steps Before Falling Asleep

1. Put aside any negativity or worries of the day.

2. Relax your entire body with an inner sense of peace.

3. Using present tense: visualize, believe, feel relieved and appreciative for having whatever it is you wish to manifest in your life.

4. Maintain your intention until it goes with you into your sleep.

Chapter Seven

Energy Exercises

Spiraling Energy

The rest of this book will show you that when we spiral subtle energy, the power potential which we access increases exponentially. The path of this energy is intrinsically of a spiral makeup. As soon as we create them, these spirals or vortices act as antennas that automatically pick up our intentions of *already having received,* which immediately goes to the hyper-dimensional realm of the omnipotent mind from where the replacement of the existing unwanted reality will be pulled into manifestation. This access to the timeless realm of the omnipotent mind occurs because *a torsion field is forced to exist between the spiraling vortex of your intention and the opposing spiraling vortex of the waveform belonging to the existing reality.* The potential energy of both reach the timeless state through this circuit. The circuit then reciprocates by instantaneously "pushing out" into realization the engineer's intention. The waveform of the original unwanted reality remains, and is unrealized in the timeless realm of the subconscious.

Not only are all of our energetic centers themselves spiraling vortices, but so are the trillions of DNA molecules within our bodies, each which allow the omnipotent mind to retrieve and fulfill our intentions. In fact everything that exists is composed of waveforms which spiral energy. Therefore, we must properly qualify our intentions in order to thus make them available for such retrieval, as taught earlier in this book.

The benefits of energy exercises are many. A heightened sensitivity to the activity of subtle energy allows every part of your body to communicate with every other part on a cellular level in order to allow optimal function and healing. Energy exercises will increase your connection with the rest of the material universe, and they will initiate and expand your spiritual development. They will accelerate your ability to unite with your divine nature and accomplish the miraculous.

There are many energy exercises that are worth practicing. The one I am about to describe is one that I've formulated to be more complete than the ones I've tried from other modalities. It actually follows the same energetic flow as that of the *waveparticle*. This is the natural flow that our bodies, as a whole unit, emit on a quantum level as well. This is in keeping with the holographic principle which states that the same elements seen in a whole unit will be seen in all of the parts of that whole.

Exercise Eight — The Quantum Wave

1. Find a quiet place. Either stand or lay down (do not sit), then close your eyes. (You may want to lay down when doing this exercise the first few times until you get the hang of it).

2. Using the power of your imagination, form a large brilliantly-white ball of light beneath your feet. This ball should be as wide as the widest part of your body.

3. Start spinning the ball clockwise like a top and as fast as you can with its rotational axis in line with your body.

4. Move the spinning ball upward through your feet all the way up just past the top of your head. Inhale as it moves upward.

5. From the point that it leaves the top of your head make the ball revolve downward and *around* your body without letting it touch your body. You can still sense it, feeling its proximity. Exhale as it moves downward.

6. When it reaches around your feet, position it beneath your feet as in the beginning of this exercise and continue to repeat the above steps until it becomes easy for you to do.

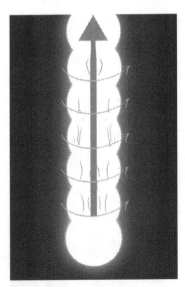

The Quantum Wave: Steps 2-4

If you begin to feel very uncomfortable, then stop for the moment and relax until you feel better. What you are feeling is your body's unfamiliarity with its true natural energy flow which has experienced resistance in a multitude of ways throughout your life. The natural flow has been interrupted and misdirected for so long that your body's readjustment is now making you feel the difference. Polishing the energy field with pure white light can also have an emotionally cathartic effect on you. So, start off with a few minutes at a time if necessary, and increase the time you spend doing the exercise until the uneasiness disappears and you begin to become empowered.

Advanced Quantum Wave

If you have been doing well with the previous exercise, you may move on to put its advanced form into practice. The physical body, being an extension of Source, is only a part of an even greater whole. This exercise utilizes the holographic principle in an even more expansive way by considering our entire universe as the whole of which our bodies are just a part of. This exercise helps us realign ourselves with the entirety of the cosmos.

Exercise Nine

1. Begin by performing the previous exercise for a few circulations.

2. With the ball positioned above your head begin to revolve the ball downward, but this time the ball will revolve *a few feet farther away from your body,* widening its periphery around your body.

3. When it reaches the level of your feet, it repositions itself just beneath your feet.

4. After moving it up through your body again to just above your head, revolve it downward again at an even *wider* periphery around your body.

5. Continue this way until the periphery reaches the very depth of the universe.

6. When the above has become easy for you, then instead of the ball returning to your feet, when it reaches the level of your feet, allow it to *continue revolving down to the depth of the universe way beneath your feet.*

7. Once it has reached there, make it shoot straight back up toward your feet, up through your entire body, out of your head, and straight up toward the other end of the universe above your head.

8. Once it has reached the depth of the universe over your head, then make it revolve downward again near the outer edges of the entire universe to its depth beneath your feet. Continue this way, shooting it up straight through your body, and so on.

[If your breath cannot seem to stay in sync with the raising and lowering of the ball, this is quite alright. Eventually your proficiency will be such that the ball will align itself with the breath. The main objective is the movement and the sensing of the ball of light, making it flow properly.]

Magnetic Entanglement

In chapter four you were encouraged to feel the activity of subtle energy in your own body. *Magnetic Entanglement* expands this ability even more. At the same time it increases your ability to attract to you anything whatsoever. You become conscious of the scope of your attractive quality by magnetically entangling yourself with all that surrounds you. The more far-reaching your ability to feel becomes, the more you can attract and influence that which is within that periphery.

Performing this exercise requires that you maintain a pleasant state of emotion and think of nothing in particular other than the performance of the exercise. Maintaining good emotions safeguards you in case unbidden thoughts do surface in your mind. Such spontaneous thoughts should be held at a distance as you remain unaffected by them.

Never begin any of these exercises unless you are in a good mood, which if at this point you cannot induce within yourself, you haven't practiced the earlier exercises thoroughly enough. I suggest that you do so.

Exercise Ten

1. Perform Exercise Two which is found in chapter four.

2. With eyes still closed, become aware of and feel your heart region and expand this feeling a few feet beyond your body simultaneously in all directions (like an expanding bubble). Maintain this for at least five minutes.

3. Begin to expand this even further, feeling the entire room you are in. Maintain this also for five minutes.

4. Expand it even further and further until you can include the far reaches of the universe *in all directions simultaneously.*

5. As you maintain this awareness, begin to feel the emotion of unconditional love emanating from your heart area, allowing the feeling to fill the entire universe around you. Feel this emotion as an extension of your being. You can incorporate other positive emotions and intentions in accordance with what you want to achieve with this particular exercise.

The surrounding bio-electric/magnetic field is the drawing board of your reality. You are adjusting your world by re-designing it in line with what brings you true happiness as it is defined by you. The longer you maintain this field around you, whatever becomes a part of the field will become that much more affected and changed by the quality and intention you hold within your field. Appreciate the beautiful artwork you are creating.

Magnetic Entanglement is the process of consciously polarizing yourself, a living magnet, with the universe. The very act of extending your reach outward with your intent, consciously *entangles* you with everything you contact or which enters your field of awareness. You activate the latent magnetic connection with your surroundings. This entanglement is limited only by the extent of your reach, the outer periphery of your reach. By polarizing yourself with the entire Universe you eliminate such limitations. Whatever you wish to be done, will be done.

This is an expansion of consciousness, an extension of your beingness and of your awareness. It helps support your belief of the omnipresent quality that is already inherent within you. This understanding and acceptance opens up your eyes to what you are truly capable of. Your potential seems to be less of a theory that you read in a book about quantum mechanics—you actually experience it. The more of this field that you are aware of, the more your power of belief can come into play and bring about desired effects from within your expansion into that new sphere of awareness.

Addendum A

The Practice of Energy Healing

There exists numerous energy healing modalities. The information which you've already read in this book should make it very easy for you to understand the underlying basis of how these modalities work.

When we watch the outward methods of various spiritual healers, all we see are the differences of the waving of the hands or whatever their particular rituals may consist of. On the other hand, whatever is going on subjectively, the part we *don't* see, is what truly determines the success (or failure) of their healing sessions. Without being given comprehensive instruction on the *subjective* methods employed, the *outer* rituals and labels can be quite deceptive to someone who is trying to learn these healing methods. Even after a student has been thoroughly taught a particular modality, it is possible for such student to become biased toward that modality, believing it is *the* modality partly due to the student having experienced a certain degree of success in performing healings, and also partly due to a certain *loyalty to the method*. In doing this the student is thereby missing the opportunity to have a more comprehensive understanding of energy healing dynamics by adopting a more advantageous eclectic approach. What I present to you is the condensed result of my research using that very approach.

Resonance

The entire universe is a perfect and harmonious creation of the omnipotent mind. This includes the human body. When "sick" or "injured," the body has an enormous capacity to heal itself. A person who continues to be sick is unable to *out-picture* the sickness, regardless of how the person became sick. The truth of the body's perfection is somehow prevented from being exhibited, and a corresponding inharmonious energy field will be emanating from the person's body.

Energetic, or resonant healing occurs when the cause of the sickness is bypassed due to the *complete* out-picturing of it, thereby opening the way for the omnipotent mind to do what it needs to do in order to make the healing happen instantaneously. This occurs when the overpowering field of the healer interacts with the sick person's field, allowing it to resonate on a vibrational frequency where illness and injury does not exist.

When something resonates with something else, a harmonious and synchronous relationship between the two is established. Tuning forks, piano wires, menstruating women living in proximity to each other, are just a few of the more well-known examples of the phenomenon of resonance. The energy field emanating from a sick person's body has a particular vibration which must be readjusted back to a harmonious state in order for the person to make a recovery. One way this can be done is by the synchronization of his or her vibrational frequency with the energy field of a healing practitioner that puts out *a vibration of perfection*. When such a field interacts with the sick person's field, the inharmonious vibrational frequency becomes influenced in direct correspondence to the vibration of the harmonious one. It will resonate with the higher vibration. For this to be a complete healing resonance, in no way is the lower frequency to have any effect upon the higher frequency. Any resistance by the person to be healed must not be greater than the healer's level of awareness of perfection maintained throughout the healing session.

An apt analogy is when you vividly remember an event that you experienced with a friend years ago, yet your friend cannot recall that it ever happened. There is no resonance happening between the both of you with regard to that specific memory. As you relate the event to jog your friend's memory, your friend tries to relive the moments of that forgotten memory. The more you fill in the gaps, the closer your friend comes to remembering until your friend finally lights up and says *Yes, I remember now!* Your friend is now convinced that he or she *did* experience the particular event, and nobody can convince your friend otherwise. Your minds are now resonating in agreement with each other. This is very similar to how resonance of our subtle energy fields work—it is a *reminding* of our original native state of perfection.

In our analogy, if you are unable to give enough details in your description, or if your friend for some reason is actively resistant to remembering the event, then your friend may not remember, or may remember a few days or a month or two later. In a healing session, the more complete you are in reminding the other person's energy field of how it should be vibrating, the more likely you are of assisting the individual towards their own effective healing. This is why healings, as with any other category of manifestation, can occur either over a prolonged period of time or instantaneously.

In addition, there are many things that practitioners can do to adulterate the process needed for healing to occur if they're not careful. *Doubt*, for example, no matter how slight, will tend to nullify a healing.

The following sections give details of varying methods of healing that are very effective.

The Healing Mindset

Address yourself first before attempting to ever heal anybody. This involves being able to understand and effectively apply the information mentioned in earlier chapters of this book. If you have thoroughly done the exercises given, then the healing mindset should be relatively easy for you.

You know you have the healing mindset when you approach a "sick" person and you don't *see* that person as being sick. You see perfection *despite any appearance to the contrary*. The disease, condition, injury, etc., does not concern you at all. You know that lying just beneath the veneer or picture of sickness is a perfectly healthy individual. You dismiss and out-picture the lie by fully accepting the perfection. You believe in it whole-heartedly.

The appearance of sickness is a lie you must see beyond in order to convince the person's energy field of the truth of the body's perfection. Such a shift in belief is what removes the veneer. Just as you've learned to see the end result in order to produce a manifestation, the mindset of *knowing* that the person is well even *before* the session, is required in order for true healing to take place. Any other thought you entertain which belies that requisite belief is the result of you not having addressed your ability to see a perfected universe as was taught in an earlier chapter. The more you are *concerned* about the person's condition, the less *effective* you will be as a healer.

It is essential not to be deterred by symptoms and doubts; instead, focus on the ultimate goal of restoring the person to a state of good health, balance, relaxation, and strength. Maintain a steadfast commitment to the correct thoughts, holding them more firmly in mind than the other person clings to incorrect ones.

As a matter of fact, a true healer doesn't consider himself a healer at all, because as far as the practitioner is concerned, *there is nothing to heal*. The practitioner is someone that maintains the truth and reality that there is no sickness, no injury, and no disease.

The practitioner is not fooled by appearances of imperfection. They don't *buy into* the illusion of distinction. As a matter of fact, he doesn't even see the situation as "no-sickness," but as "only healthy," keeping it in the positive-tense, not the negative-tense. He only knows and maintains the truth of perfect health and its supportive feelings which are radiantly expanded to encompass and embody the reality of the sick person. Though a misnomer, this is the healer's mindset that must be practiced and adopted until the concept becomes true for you.

Presence Healing

When you are in the presence of someone who is suffering from a certain condition, the *apparency* of such a condition can be treated in the following way:

1. Make sure the person is either sitting up or lying down, not standing up.

2. Sit or stand near the person, all the while maintaining the healing mindset as described above.

3. Expand the energy from your heart center large enough to entirely encompass both you and the other person.

4. As you maintain the healing mindset, the quality of the expanded heart energy will be of an overwhelming joy, appreciation, and relief or satisfaction that the person is a perfectly healthy human being.

5. Continue to focus on and maintain the belief and feeling as outlined above, allowing for no interruption.

6. There will be an indication that something about the person has changed. This can show up instantaneously or

may surface after some time. Regardless of what you may or may not witness, let nothing surprise you, even if the person enters an altered state of consciousness, which is not uncommon. Positive changes are happening.

7. Maintain the above requisite subjective stance even after the end of the session and go about the rest of your day.

Well-formulated intention, along with magnified sensitivity to subtle energy, will determine the practitioner's ability to out-picture the other person's energy field, and thereby having the person's field resonate with your own. You will be able to magnify your sensitivity to subtle energy if you have thoroughly practiced emotion/feeling/breathing exercises like the ones taught in the earlier chapters.

Hands-On Healing

This method allows your *hands* to create torsion fields within the energetic field of the person. These torsion fields interact with the "sick" or "injured" person's field, allowing for desired changes to occur which originate within the vacuum created by, and at the center of, the torsion fields. It does not require you to *accumulate* energy for the purpose of *sending* it through your hands and into the body of the sick person. The healing itself occurs by means of introducing the vibrational field of the omnipotent mind. This is the method:

1. Perform steps one through four as outlined in *Presence Healing*.

2. With hands and wrists relaxed as much as possible, palms facing the other person, have them scan the person's energetic field in order to *intuitively find* (with no active

thought of your own) two separate spots in the field, one for each hand, to which they are drawn. A very subtle and invisible connection is *felt* to have been created *between the two hands* when the spots are found. The areas may be on the body itself, around and near the body, or a combination of the two. Take care not to tense the hands when this connection is made. (Do not expect or attempt for your conscious mind to be involved in this magnetic selection. The selection that the hands have made may seem random to you, but they are never wrong, and you must accept it as such.)

3. Once positioned, feel from the center of the palms of both hands, vortices of magnetic energy swirling in a counter-rotational fashion in relation to each other. It should feel as if the vortices are trying to pull the hands toward each other, thereby making the connection between them even stronger without it actually pulling your hands together. Maintain this connection within the energy field that you have expanded from your heart center.

4. After you receive an *indicator of change*, such as a distinct fluctuation of energy or an energy shift, you may then have one or both hands find a different position as in step two, and repeat the process until you feel that the session has accomplished its purpose.

As the mind is totally occupied in *taking a measurement* (interpreting what it has its attention on), unobstructed changes occur in accordance with the intention that you maintain in your heart because the intention is inextricably *linked* with the taking of the measurement. The vacuum of the torsion fields created between your hands allow optimal intentions to access the vibrational field of the omnipotent mind via the Reciprocal

Circuit, thereby resonating with it and producing the physical reality effect of a healthy person.

Distance Healing

Being far away from a person that is in need of healing does not prevent you from being as effective in a healing session with that person than if that person were right in front of you. Of course, you must somehow know and identify who the person is in order to establish the energetic connection required in a healing session. Once the connection is established, then the two previous healing methods can be performed as outlined. Some of the different ways that this connection can be established are as follows:

- Simply *think* of the person.

- Visualize the person in front of you as a *thought-form* in real-time, actually seeing the person and interacting with the thought-form as if it was the actual person, which for all intents and purposes *is* the actual person.

- Conduct the session while you are on the *phone* or *online* with them.

- Have a *picture* of them in front of you.

- Have a personal *item* of theirs in front of you.

- Have someone who personally *knows* the individual tell you who the person is: name, relationship, description.

- Any *combination* of the above.

Being conscious of the person during the session requires that you absolutely know that an energetic connection is effectively established. *There can be no doubt about this.* The power of the mind transcends all of space and time, and therefore distance as well.

Addendum B

Serpentine Power

The subject of mind power would not be complete without a discussion of what esotericists call the *serpentine fire, serpentine force,* or *serpentine power.* The sanskrit word *kundalini* is the feminine form of the word which means *circular* or *coiled.* Hindu and Buddhist teachings explain that *kundalini* is a force of subtle energy which coils itself like a serpent and lies dormant at the base of the human spine. When awoken, or activated, this serpent uncoils itself, and extends itself, winding up and around the core of the *sushumna* to reconnect the base of the spine with the top of the head, activating all of the *chakras* consecutively along the way.

This is a basic description of the process which results in spiritual enlightenment to the individual.

Throughout my years of research I have found a particular subject, in connection with *kundalini*, surfacing time and again. This would seem to happen more often when the source of my findings were written further back in time or if the writing was more difficult to come across. There was a common theme that I couldn't ignore given the fact that they all came from very unrelated sources and eras. At first the subject seemed obscure until I continued to be confronted with the same subject conveyed in either different terminology or explanatory angles.

To sum up my findings I will use the term *vital power* or *sex-power*. Don't assume that you know what this term means until I've explained its true significance. The material you have read so far in this book can stand on its own insofar as it is highly effective in engineering your own reality when it is properly applied. This additional material not only adds further understanding to the use of our omnipotent mind, but offers an additional avenue to further explore and increase your ability to utilize subtle energy force exponentially. This information can be used to enhance the techniques you've already learned. I have added it to the back of this book because it is extremely powerful, and only people who have practiced the previous techniques *thoroughly* can begin to safely apply what they are about to read in this section.

What do I mean by sex-power? Within our bodies is a natural urge which in our society has become distorted, misunderstood, and even corrupted by the very thoughts that we attach to it. The power of this urge is so vital, it has the ability to be directed toward the procreative act, thereby bringing forth new life. This is natural and proper when both parties agree to this outcome. We also find extreme enjoyment in the act itself. But, as you shall see, this very urge not only has its place in the obtaining of enlightenment through *kundalini* activation, but it can also shorten our path significantly to realizing omnipotence.

It is no mistake that this energy is described as a coil. Consider the many ways this specific design manifests in relation to energy:

- Our genetic code itself has a coil-like shape to it.

- The word *rib* that is used in reference to Adam's rib (which is removed in order to form Eve out of it) has a literal translation which means *flattened spiral.*

- Specialized healers, particularly those focusing on tissue regeneration, possess an entire spectrum of colors within their energy fields. The intricate red spectrum they exhibit at times mirrors the structure of the double helix in the genetic code.

- The movement performed by the *dancing dervishes* of the Sufi sect of Islam, in order to obtain union with divine energy, is composed of the spinning of their bodies at very high speeds as if creating a sort of vortex.

- The form taken by quantum energy when it expresses itself as a wave appears as such a vortex.

- The chakras and acupuncture points are energetic areas within the body that spin at very high speeds.

- The story of *Job* points out that when God finally speaks to him, He does so out of a whirlwind.

- Fibonacci Sequence and Spirals: The Fibonacci sequence, a series of numbers where each number is the sum of the two preceding ones, is closely related to spiral patterns found in nature. The spiral patterns, such as the golden spiral, are seen in shells, galaxies, and other natural forms.

- Torus Energy Fields: The torus, a geometric shape resembling a doughnut or a smoke ring, is associated with energy flow and dynamics. The human energy field operates in a toroidal pattern, with energy circulating in and around the body in a torus-like fashion.

- Magnetic Fields and Lines: Magnetic fields often create a spiral or coil-like pattern. Magnetic field lines from a permanent magnet form circles that are like layers that come out from one end, curve around, and go back into the other end, making a spiral shape.

The infinite possibilities that a quantum wave represents can be observed in an uncontrolled manner in tornadoes, hurricanes, and in the description of black holes. At the very center of these natural vortices occur phenomena that would seem quite bizarre if not looked at within the context of the power of subtle energy force and its connection to a realm beyond time and space. Within this very center is the *absolute balance*, infinite equilibrium which allows for anything to be possible.

The aftermaths of tornadoes have revealed evidence of the seemingly "impossible." Pieces of wood that have merged with other pieces of wood when they should have easily shattered on contact. A rod of metal that shot through a glass window was found fused with the unbroken window when it should have shattered it. Instead, the part in contact with the glass actually became part of the glass! These and many other anomalies have been found.

A team of Russian scientists headed by Gariaev found that DNA activated by waves have the ability to manipulate the space matrix, generating minute electromagnetic wormholes of a subquantum nature. These DNA-activated wormholes, exhibiting energy signatures akin to Einstein-Rosen bridges discovered near black holes, serve as links between distinct regions in the multiverse, enabling the transmission of data beyond the confines of space-time. The theorized concept suggests that even after the removal of DNA, torsion waves from beyond space and time persistently flow through the activated wormholes.

My point in highlighting this information is to emphasize the importance that this spiral-like energy has in its controlled use in our lives. The sex-urge associated with the *kundalini* coil, and of which we are familiar with within our bodies, can be used to our advantage because of its vital connection to the realization of our omnipotent mind.

Conservation of Sex-Energy

The thoughts we entertain contribute to the feelings we experience. When I say conservation of sex-energy, the physical aspect is almost a peripheral aspect of what I mean. The teachings I have come across have emphasized a need to avoid the expenditure of sex-energy that occurs by means of the sex act itself, but it is not only the sex act itself that concerns us. In controlling our thoughts with regard to this sex urge, we build up a sort of battery within ourselves. If we were to simply obstruct the flow of energy by not engaging in any sex acts, we would only be holding back a flow that is still seeking to be expressed in one particular direction. The longer it is suppressed, the stronger the urge transforms into lust. I don't propose that we stop engaging in healthy sexual conduct. What I am saying is that our bodies and minds have been accustomed to one avenue of release of this powerful energy when there is another way that it can flow to our benefit, a way that we are not ordinarily accustomed to.

I can tell you that when I began to conserve this energy and maintain the *attitude* that was in line with the purpose of such conservation, my imaginative faculties became extraordinarily powerful, even in the dream-state I was able to see the most vivid scenarios which I had no problem remembering upon awakening. My sensitivity to subtle energy force was multiplied, and my ability to induce the required emotions within me became remarkably easy. The longer I didn't think about the subject of sexual release as I normally knew it, the easier it was for me to not engage in it. I knew that once I began dwelling on the satisfaction-factor of sex, the energy would begin to divert toward that expression and lust soon would be the result. Once lust enters the picture, it will take all of the mental strength you can muster to become the victor over it.

Determination is of prime necessity in this particular area. You must whole-heartedly enter the spirit of this practice in order to succeed. Even if you succumb at any given point, this does not preclude you from starting anew and becoming even more determined and vigilant than before. With regard to our internal dialogue, the most effective way I've found is to *change the subject*, so to speak. When you begin to initiate a thought that would lead down the road of physical sexual release, nip it right in the bud and think a new thought and divert your attention! This is very effective. You are not necessarily adopting this practice for any religious reasons, but you are applying a method that has existed for a very long time and has been misinterpreted by many religious observers to be of a moral value only, when it is much more. Many sacred writings explain this, yet over time religious slants have obscured its true benefit. To be sure, promiscuity will tend to nullify your ability to produce results with the power of the mind.

The way to begin this practice properly is by starting little by little. In terms of time, start with a couple of days, then keep extending it to work your way to a week, then a couple of weeks, a month, a month and a half, two months, etc., all the while continuing to perform the exercises you learned in this book. In other words, decide how much you are reasonably willing to do and then stick to it. You may be an individual who can do this much easier than others, if so, more power to you. With regard to your stream of thoughts, resolve not to think about or seek out anything that would entice you in the physical expression of the sex-urge. If you feel the urge rise on its own within your body *do not attach any corresponding thoughts to it!* Do not fantasize or visualize thought-forms that prod the sex-urge to flow in that direction. This new mindset allows the energy to be available for the purpose of enlightenment, creating your reality, and accessing the fifth dimension. The key is not to feel that you are forcing yourself to do something that you don't want to do. This would negate the purpose, and the result is that the energy itself will be affected by this very attitude. *Energy follows thought* is the axiom that will prove to be so true in this context.

Let me be clear on this: it is not enough to stop yourself from engaging in sexual pleasures resulting in orgasm, it is also necessary to *consciously regulate your accompanying thoughts and intentions.* Your thoughts should not be inclined toward the physical anticipation of sexual pleasure. The reason the thought may continue to surface is because it has become a habitual inclination to think in that direction, thereby resulting in the strong desire to engage in it. As mentioned earlier, the mind can train itself to accept new habits that the *I* initiates. Throughout this practice you will develop a new attitude and disposition concerning this. It in turn will actually result in a healthier body and a more alert mind, though these benefits are peripheral to our purposes.

I recall one individual named Kay who began this practice in what I perceived was an incomplete application of it. Kay was an individual that normally exhibited an overindulgent sexual drive and interest. Kay's desire to acquire the powerful benefits that the practice can bestow gave Kay enough impetus to last an entire week without engaging in any type of sexual release. At the end of the week Kay said to me *I couldn't take it anymore. I had to!* The problem was that whenever Kay felt an impulse, the stream of thought was not immediately diverted by Kay, no doubt indulging in erotic fantasies. This is tantamount to someone who is fasting, yet thinks about all the food he or she is missing out on: *Oh, those recipes I will try when I finish my fast!* Kay simply had forcefully denied the body sexual release until finally giving in. This is incorrect and potentially harmful to the mind and body.

Therefore, make sure you are determined and that your plan is set in place. Understand that obstacles will come your way and be prepared with the right mental disposition. If not, you will be overpowered quite easily. The energy you are dealing with is intensely active, so treat it as such. If you had to handle a live wire of high-voltage electricity, would you be carefree about it? I would hope not. Lightning is not as powerful as the power within you!

Addendum C

The Caduceus Within the Cross

The esoteric meaning of the caduceus and the cross are worth elaborating on because they can prove very useful in understanding and remembering the practical application of the principles outlined in this book.

Both the caduceus and the cross are usually viewed as distinct symbols that carry different meanings, but there are principles more profound that bring them together. The cross is a true symbol of *Yoga*, where it has often been so described as the reconciling of the human soul *below* with the divine spirit *above*. The caduceus is the staff or wand of *Hermes Mercurius Trismegistus* whose most fundamental teaching, as it is found in his *Emerald Tablet*, proclaims *As it is Above, So it is Below*. Contained within the combining of these symbols you will find the key to unlocking the power of your omnipotent mind. It is as follows:

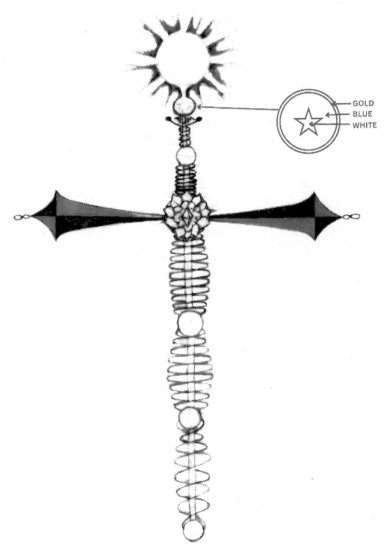

GOLD
BLUE
WHITE

The Caduceus within the Cross

The entire cross itself is a symbol of *you*. The *horizontal* beam reflects the same horizontal position of a timeline which proceeds from past to present to future. This particular beam therefore represents the world of duality where vibrations of subtle energy have become manifested as physical reality expressed in space and time. These manifestations consist of both desired and undesired experiences. This is also where the physical body resides in linear time.

Within the *vertical* beam is found the caduceus, a gravitational vortex of potentiality where all unmanifested vibrations of subtle energy exist. This spiraling vortex is what I have been referring to throughout this book as the *Reciprocal Circuit*. This vortex is composed of the polarized sub-conscious and the unpolarized superconscious aspects of the mind which function *outside* the limits of space and time. The entire vertical beam from top to bottom corresponds with the non-physical chakra system composed of smaller distinct vortices that are aligned with the spinal column and the brain.

At the very center of the vortex, running through all of the chakras, is a central channel that represents the *vacuum* of the vortex. This unpolarized central channel is an extension of the highest chakra which pertains to the omnipotent superconscious mind of the divine spirit—the higher self. In your purest and most complete state of being, this *self* is not just a part of you, it actually *is* you. Through its optimal expression, it has the effects of health and regeneration on the physical body, hence the use of the caduceus as the symbol commonly used by physicians and the medical community.

The outer part of the vortex, encircling the central channel, are the dual-natured spiraling vortices of polarized energy (*ida* positive and *pingala* negative) which have a suboptimal influence on the vibratory frequency of all the chakras, except the highest one. These two waveforms represent resistance, and pertain to the process of the subconscious mind of the false lower self, and which is the reason we forget our true relationship to the omnipotent creator, the *All in all*. The greater resistance we have, the stronger the opposition will exist between the two spiraling vortices. Without resistance between them, the unison of the vortices activate the unpolarized energy of the central channel, which becomes the dominant vibration that is emanated. Both aspects always exist, but only one can be dominantly active at any given point in time.

The lower self is not who you really are, but is the resulting frequency within the chakras due to the vibrational accumulation of all the polarized impressions that come from duality-consciousness. Through its suboptimal expression, it has the effects of disease and degeneration on the physical body. Since duality disguises our true beingness, this bi-polar aspect of the vortex is also analogous to a mirror that whenever we look into it to see what we really look like, the true image of the higher self is distorted by the mirror's duality-altered surface, reflecting back the illusory image of the dual-natured lower self (hence the symbol of the *dual*-horned devil, the origin of lies). From this viewpoint, we also see an altered version of what our world consists of, and it is very convincing. Fortunately, as you'll see shortly, we can remove the distortion and see beyond the deception.

From our vantage point, the most important part of the cross is where both beams intersect. This is the point which corresponds with the powerful heart chakra, the emotional center and portal through which physical reality *interacts* with the non-physical energetic activity that is represented by the vertical beam. Both polarized and unpolarized aspects of the vortex are thus accessible through this chakra in present time. Additionally, by interacting with non-linear time through present time, the past and future can likewise be influenced.

The interaction between the physical and the non-physical is the result of a feedback loop called the *Reciprocal Circuit*. All energy must go somewhere, therefore when we choose to

140

place our attention on something, the vibrations of thought and emotion which are thereby produced, begin to circulate along the Reciprocal Circuit, where they are automatically pulled into this vortex and remain (unbeknownst to us) as vibrational *non-physical* realities until the circuit is completed, resulting in the vibrational reality becoming a physical reality. This can happen in an instant, or it can take years—it's up to you.

The gravitational pull through the Reciprocal Circuit of the vortex is made possible by means of the principle of *Like Attracts Like,* a universal principle which is as active in this vortex of potentiality as it is in our physical reality. Therefore, all vibrations which we radiate, depending on their resonant quality, will be attracted by, and flow with the aspect of the vortex that pertains to either the higher self or the lower self. When a particular vibratory flow completes a full circulation, it returns to present-time physical reality as the physical manifestation of the essence of the vibration involved.

The energy which is transferred from present time consciousness to the vortex does so instantaneously because such transference occurs *outside* the limits of space and time. This is where all of our vibrations will and must go before they can potentially return to become manifestations in physical reality. The Reciprocal Circuit is the road traveled by our vibrations to first become true in this vortex, and then to become true in physical reality. It is a highway of vibrations that is ever-active, bringing you a steady stream of the physical reality that you perpetually experience.

On any given subject, the flow of vibrational energy with the least amount of resistance completes the Reciprocal Circuit. When, in present time, our undeviating attention on any given subject allows its energy to equate and fully harmonize with the existing energy that has already become true *vibrationally,* its *resistance* has been removed. Fully resonating in this way *pulls* the current of vibrational energy from its state of timelessness into physical manifestation where it freely flows to complete the circuit. This will occur the moment the vibrational energy *dominates* the energy upholding the existing physical reality, thereby *replacing* it. Depending on how we focus our attention, whether with the eyes of *duality* or the eye of *singularity*, will determine if the circuit results in a suboptimal or optimal manifestation.

Why then, does our relentless attention on what we desire sometimes result in the manifestation of what is *undesired?* This is due to the fact that *desired* manifestations come from the *unpolarized* aspect of the vortex, and we get what we *don't desire* when we vibrate in resonance with the *polarized* aspect of the vortex. More specifically, not believing in something desired, or believing in something undesired, does *not* stimulate an unpolarized vibration, but a *polarized* one. A polarized vibration occurs because *doubting something desired does not feel good to you,* neither does *believing something undesired.* This evokes a polarized emotional vibration, which in turn results in a manifestation which contradicts your true desire. The presence of resistance exists because of the awareness of what doesn't feel good, which can only be experienced by bi-polar consciousness.

With bi-polar consciousness, the undesired thing that is already seen in physical reality may feel truer than what is desired. This results in a desire that has the resistance of *unbelief* attached to it, while your belief does not resist what already exists, though you do not desire it. As the result of such resistance, the desire will remain vibrationally suspended, stuck midway on the Reciprocal Circuit as a mere potentiality until, by your inattention to the *trueness* of the undesired physical reality, its resistance is weakened enough to allow the non-physical vibration to complete its full course towards the desired manifestation and replace the existing reality. Likewise, an unrealized desire will manifest in physical reality when, by your continual attention to its *trueness*, it becomes vibrationally strong enough to overcome, dominate, and replace any existing physical reality which contradicts it.

142

The work that removes resistance is accomplished at the beams' intersection, the location of the *heart chakra*, which is the powerful center and emanation point of our emotions, feelings, and desires that we experience in present time. The quality and persistence of the emotion felt at this crucial juncture determines whether or not our vibrations will result in our desired manifestations. Just as there are emotions which assist our *desired* manifestations by vibrating in resonance with the desire, there are also emotions that assist our *undesired* manifestations by vibrating in contradiction to our desire. In order to manifest desires which are to our benefit, though, the *continued attention* must be maintained only on vibrations compatible with the uni-polar omnipotent mind of the higher self.

The stronger the belief in the desire, the stronger compatibility will exist between our emotions and our higher self. By fostering thoughts of your desires, powerful emotions will also surface. These will be emotions that resonate with—and strengthen belief in—the very desires that you foster. The reason this happens is because when you focus on what you desire, you are also resonating with the vibrations of your higher self who has already made your desire a vibrational truth, thereby making the inflow of supportive emotion an increased connection with your higher self. The thoughts and emotions which resonate with this aspect of the vortex will always be the source of every beneficial result you experience in your life.

Your higher self is infinitely intelligent and knows what is best for you, what will truly make you happy, and how to make it happen most efficiently—even if *you* haven't figured it out yet. This is because whenever you vibrate *directly* in a bi-polar direction, you always *indirectly* influence the uni-polar aspect of the vortex. In this way, no matter how you vibrate, your higher self will "pick up" (and immediately make a vibrational truth out of), for instance, your indirect desire for financial security if you ever had a direct fear of poverty. But if you continue to vibrate that fear by your attention to it, poverty will not be ruled out from your life until you begin and maintain focused attention on, and resonate with, the existing vibrational truth of financial security that was indirectly and simultaneously formed in the uni-polar aspect of the vortex.

Your higher self also knows what you consider to be your ideal mate, your ideal job/career/lifestyle, your ideal encounters and interactions, your ideal life as a whole, your ideal anything and everything. These are available to you because they have been made true *in potentiality*. Resonate with these truths and they will flow into your life.

When your direct attention stabilizes at the top chakra *(the chakra that is completely untouched by the bi-polar aspect of the vortex, and of which the central channel is a direct extension)*, an indirect event begins to occur all the way at the bottom base of the central channel, where the awakening of a pure form of subtle energy is magnetically drawn upwards by the higher self through the central channel, penetrating all of the chakras with a purifying influence, until finally connecting with the topmost chakra. Three levels— or outer layers—of the central channel will be traversed before reaching the innermost tunnel within the central channel which allows the finest vibration of this pure energy to travel upwards, and thereby make such a connection.

Go in through the Narrow Gate

This is when pure *consciousness* unites with pure *energy*. On its way upward, polarized blockages of resistance dissolve, transcending the bi-polar lower self along with its illusory dual nature. This is the process of *singularity-consciousness* (super-consciousness) traveling up the central channel, and clearing away the vibrational distortion which was formed in the chakras by the bi-polar aspect of the vortex, allowing an undistorted reflection of the higher self. This is the unfolding of the individual's awareness of his true nature, and awareness of his relationship with divine power.

The connecting of the top and bottom of this vortex through the central channel is the true *yoga* of divine union where the feminine aspect of pure energy (*shakti*) becomes one with the masculine aspect of pure consciousness (*shiva*), and in the process, where the uniting of the bi-polar opposites within the vortex occur as well. Singularity-consciousness and duality-consciousness cannot be simultaneously active, *you cannot serve two masters.*

Achieving this union the *first* time is a challenge. *Maintaining* it is quite another. It may require several attempts over time, but persistence will eventually result in a properly closed circuit (*ouroborus:* the end is the beginning). Stabilized attention at the top chakra (*sahasrara*) means embodying divine qualities *unconditionally,* with no resistance whatsoever. When all reasons not to love, not to enjoy, not to appreciate, and not to see beauty in all of your life experiences are totally disregarded, and you embody such qualities anyway, you are on your way to achieving such a union.

Device: The symbol of the cross has sometimes been depicted with a radiant rose at its point of intersection. That is what you want your thoughts, emotions, and manifestations to be like:

- Beautiful

- Pleasant

- Flourishing

- Joyful

- Inspiring

- Fragrant

- Full of Life and Love

- Uplifting and Connected to Life Source.

That is where the focus of your attention should be in order to live the life you've always wanted.

Addendum D

Distinction is the Illusion

Within the bi-polar universe of duality, every wave/particle is paired up with an anti-wave/particle, spinning together in spiral fashion and in opposite directions from each other, one clockwise, the other counter-clockwise. This is *distinction* (difference, division, separation) expressed at the quantum level. Each opposing spin also produces its own respective vibrational frequency. These differing frequencies are what hold the particles apart in resistance to each other. As the particles interact, a blending of their differing vibrational frequencies results in the production of a *differential* which manifests in our material universe. In fact, the whole of our physical reality is composed entirely of manifested differentials.

Of great interest to us is the fact that *consciousness* can affect the vibrational behavior of any and all of the wave/particle pairs which are producing these differentials. The quality of that behavior is determined by how our consciousness is *focusing*. If our focus is duality-based, the resulting differential will be a suboptimal manifestation because our consciousness would not be in harmony with physical reality, it is focused on the resistance brought about by its dual nature. But when our focus is based on a consciousness that is *singularized,* we affect our reality in ways that allow us to produce differentials of optimal manifestations.

By removing polarity, the resistance is released, and you supersede the suboptimal effects that are brought about by a bi-polar consciousness. Polarity is removed by making your *eye single*, which means seeing the way our higher self sees, and attaining the uni-polar (or non-polar) state of *unconditionality*. Focusing from the vantage point of our core selves means entering a state of consciousness where there is *no awareness of distinction*, and therefore there is no resistance, allowing us to be in harmony with all of existence. When the truth of singularity is experienced, the illusion of duality dissolves: *There is no spoon*. Singularity reaches beyond the vibrational limitations of the bi-polar universe of duality, and accesses the unlimited universal consciousness of the one absolute omnipotent mind, from where only optimal manifestations are created and pulled into our physical reality. A uni-polar-conscious individual living in a bi-polar universe is what is meant by being *in the world, but not part of the world.*

Whereas bi-polar-consciousness finds *good or evil* wherever it looks, uni-polar-consciousness is an unconditional state of being that is causatively connected with everything that ever comes within its field of awareness. Everything you experience is an extension of yourself, therefore uni-polar consciousness allows you to see the qualities of your higher self *embodied* in all things because they are its extension. No opposing condition is even possible in this state of being because it is not based on the conditions that you see in physical reality, but on the way you choose to interpret those conditions. And having chosen to see through the unconditional viewpoint of your higher self, as you observe *as* your higher self, you'll base all you see on the fundamental *core* qualities that make up your essential state of being, such as *love, bliss, joy, appreciation, beauty, freedom,* and others. Your uni-polar state of consciousness is maintained as long as these core qualities are maintained—regardless of apparent conditions.

On the other hand, requiring conditions to determine our state of being takes our focus away from those core qualities, and places them on the distinction that is unavoidably inherent in those conditions to begin with, and which gives rise to separation and resistance. This is how one stays in the illusory prison of the limited world of duality.

Physical reality itself is not the illusion. *Distinction*, the result of duality-consciousness, is the actual illusion referred to as *maya*. The reason we perceive the illusion of distinction is because we deviate from the unconditional love that we experience in our true state of oneness, looking for it to appear from other than within ourselves, which is its actual place of origin. From the viewpoint of our true selves, there is no "distinction" because the viewpoint of our true selves exists in a singularized state of consciousness which, having no opposite, doesn't distinguish or differentiate itself from anything else. Hatred and anger are not qualities that your higher self possesses as "opposites" of its unconditional love, but are the result of focusing on what your higher self does *not* consist of: separation, division, and differences, which bring about suboptimal manifestations of conflict, resistance, and opposition. Neither does your higher self hold within itself *conditional* love as the opposite of unconditional love. Conditional love is simply another expression of duality-consciousness found within the lower self.

As it is our natural state, unconditional love is always available to be focused upon. The problem is that we tend to want to experience it as a *random effect* instead of being its *deliberate cause*, and we therefore find it difficult to consistently experience it. External polarized conditions are not the key to finding what you seek, but the singularized qualities of your higher self are. When we deliberately and consistently focus in order to see by means of our single eye of unconditional love, we become one with our higher self, and our optimal life can be experienced.

To Summarize:

- In order to produce optimal manifestations, you must be in the state of Uni-Polar Consciousness.

- In order to be in the state of Uni-Polar Consciousness, you must rise above bi-polar consciousness.

- In order to rise above bi-polar consciousness, you must release all resistance.

- In order to release all resistance, you must have Unconditional Love.

- In order to have Unconditional Love, you must understand all conditions.

- In order to understand all conditions, you must be *willing* to understand all conditions.

- In order to be willing to understand all conditions, you must know the *value* of understanding all conditions.

- In order to know the value of understanding all conditions, you must know how the universal law of Mind works.

Once you know how the universal law of Mind works, as this book clearly outlines for you, your desire to develop unconditional love by understanding all conditions, will grow. And it *will* grow because you now know that by developing such unconditional love, you will release the resistance that has been holding you back from the consciousness that produces the optimal manifestations you've always wanted.

Addendum E

Activating Divine Grace

What is grace? it is unmerited, undeserved, unconditional, and unqualified divine assistance, favor, or approval. It is usually understood as a granting of mercy and forgiveness, an overlooking or ignoring a wrong.

True grace comes from the omnipotent mind, not from the limited mind. Normally, we are quick to label things that we find disagreeable as *offensive, wrong*, and *unworthy of our admiration, appreciation, and love.* On the other hand, the omnipotent mind views everything as coming from itself and consisting of the same energy with the same qualitative value. Gold can be similarly molded into an innumerable amount of shapes, yet they all still consist of the same substance with the same value. The energy that everything in the universe consists of is not only the same substance, but since it originates from the fount of the divine, its value is insurmountable. This is the very energy that has come forth, and perpetually continues to come forth, from the omnipotent mind as its very creation. Any devaluation of such a creation is an alteration that does not originate from the omnipotent mind, but can only come from a viewpoint that has taken a *fall* from the grace of the higher self, resulting in a dissonance with the Source of All. The higher self is incapable of labeling anything as *wrong* or *bad.* The part of you that does so is the lower self. When this distorted view becomes sanitized of its impure vision, we are able to see what our higher self sees because we would then be seeing as our higher self.

How is this done? For instance, how can we look at a sick person and see a perfectly healthy person? The answer is that we cannot—well, at least not at the same time. It has to be one or the other. *You must definitively decide what it is that you are perceiving.* That may seem to be a very unorthodox way of thinking because we usually let reality decide for us, but even in that circumstance we are still *deciding* to surrender our power of determination, not realizing that by doing so we also abandon our infinite options.

This is the premise: Though the limited mind may see a sick person, the omnipotent mind that is your higher self does not. Only the awareness of "perfectly healthy person" can occur to such a mind. *Such a mind can never be aware of nor perceive anything negative whatsoever.* Such a mind *does perceive* though, and *always* regards every perception as positive and in line with everything you approve of, admire, enjoy, appreciate, love, etc. No matter which of our senses are involved, the higher perception is always a positive translation.

So, which is true? Is the person sick or not? The answer is that *you* must determine what is true. It does not matter what *reality* says is true. *Choice of meaning reigns over reality.* It is a choice whether to see through the eyes of your lower or higher self—but you must first come to the realization that such a choice is even possible. This is the process described by *Hermes* when he wrote *"separate the subtle from the gross."* If such separation does not take place, then you will be unable to see the power of your subjective mind to choose the truth that *becomes* reality.

The word *subtle* refers to the fine substance of consciousness which weaves and is woven within the fabric of reality. Separating that fine substance from its fabric means realizing the autonomy of the subjective consciousness, no longer allowing the *gross* objective reality to dictate truth.

This is the process: When your limited mind here *below* decides to start regarding its perceptions in the same way that your omnipotent mind *above* regards its perceptions, then you are beginning to allow that supreme power to mold everything perceived in accordance with its perfect vision. When these vibrations of perception thus resonate, the Reciprocal Circuit is permitted to flow unimpeded towards the desired manifestation. *As it is seen Above, so will it be seen Below.* You stop seeing the distorted view of your lower self. You stop seeing the person's sickness because, as far as you are concerned, it simply doesn't exist. And it doesn't exist because the perfect health *does,* and they can't both exist at the same time. If one of them is seen as true, the other is believed to be untrue. When your *perceptual decision* unveils the truth that comes from your higher self, it simultaneously exposes the illusion, thereby discontinuing the apparency of the affliction. Divine grace is simply an *allowing* of the perfect energy which has coagulated into our physical universe to be regarded and accepted *as it truly is* and for *what it truly is.* In the eyes of your higher self there is nothing to blame, find fault with, criticize, or find offensive. To reach this state of consciousness, all senses of perception must be transformed into *perpetual senses of love, joy, appreciation,* and so on—essential qualities inherent within the energy comprising the universe. This divine perception doesn't require or demand of what it sees to fulfill any special qualifications, nor does it ask for anything in return. It knows what it sees, and it is always good, perfect, and beautiful.

Many of you may feel a stirring inside which may be shouting: *Hold on, we can't just turn a blind eye to all the evil and suffering in the world!* As noble as that may be, unfortunately what it comes down to is this: *the more you see it, the more of it will you continue to see.* Divine grace is very powerful in changing the world we see, so don't underestimate what it can do. It isn't just a feel-good concept, but is much more powerful than the performance of any physical effort to change the world. This does not mean *do nothing*. Free will means that you have the *ability to decide* to do whatever you want to do. But whatever you decide *alongside* divine grace can and will make the most significant difference possible because it allows the power of the omnipotent mind to flow through and do *its* part.

Addendum F

The Uncertainty Principle

Certainty is what we feel when we have *determined* something. The opposite of certainty is uncertainty, which is what we feel when we are *unable* to determine something. Certainty and uncertainty are both *subjective*.

Werner Heisenberg presented what is called *The Uncertainty Principle*, which states as follows:

> It is impossible to determine simultaneously both
> the exact *position* and *velocity* of a particle.

When its position is determined, its velocity is uncertain because it cannot be determined precisely. Likewise, when its velocity is determined, its position is uncertain because it cannot be determined precisely. The reason for this indeterminability is because position and velocity are *complementary properties,* such as gravity and spacetime. The observation of complementary properties simply cannot be done simultaneously.

Of course, what the principle teaches us is that a resulting observation is itself dependent on what an observer's particular *choice of meaning or belief* is between the complementary properties belonging to whatever he is observing—in spite of his *desire* to observe the opposite property. The principle, as stated, seems to leave out the fact that the problem that the principle presents can only exist when the observer himself is trying to accomplish the impossible. We are left to wonder: why is this observer/measurer who *wants* to measure property *B* while accomplishing the measurement of property *A* which *prevents* him from measuring property *B*, is trying to also accomplish the measurement of *B?* If he knew that he cannot measure *B because* he is measuring *A*, then he would *stop* measuring *A* and *start* measuring *B*.

Yet, most of us attempt this all the time. We try to measure complementary properties simultaneously when such a measurement cannot be made with complete accuracy. One has to be chosen for a completely accurate measurement, and it should be the most important, with the most priority, or simply the one preferred. This is what is required in order to change our reality from the one we *don't want but have* because *we are* observing it, to the one we *desire but don't have* because *we're not* observing it. The Uncertainty Principle is another way of saying:

You cannot see something you want to see
when you are looking at something that, by looking at
it, prevents you from seeing what you want to see.

Placing your attention on something undesired prevents you from placing your attention on its desired opposite. A desire to observe something cannot be satisfied by continuing to observe its undesired opposite.

Ideally, we should only be *taking measurements of* (or "looking at") what we desire to see in life. So, for us, taking a measurement should mean maintaining our attention *only* on what is desired about something until it is the only complementary property that can be seen. Its opposite undesired property *must* disappear from your view in order for it to disappear from your life.

Printed in the United States
by Baker & Taylor Publisher Services